THE HEALTHY
Baby Meal Planner

THE HEALTHY
Baby Meal Planner

ANNABEL KARMEL

Illustrations by Nadine Wickenden

A Fireside Book
Published by Simon & Schuster Inc.
New York   London   Toronto   Sydney   Tokyo   Singapore

FIRESIDE
Simon & Schuster Building
Rockerfeller Center
1230 Avenue of the Americas
New York, New York 10020

FIRESIDE and colophon are registered trademarks
of Simon and Schuster Inc.

10 9 8 7 6 5

Library of Congress Cataloging-in-Publication Data

Karmel, Annabel.
   The healthy baby meal planner / Annabel
   Karmel.
      p. cm.
   "A Fireside book."
   "An Eddison-Sadd edition."
   Includes index.
   ISBN 0-671-75019-4
   1. Cookery (Baby foods) 2. Menus. I. Title.
TX740.K28 1992   91-15836
641.5′622–dc20   CIP

*This book is dedicated
to my children,
Nicholas and Lara
and to the memory of
my first daughter,
Natasha.*

AN EDDISON · SADD EDITION
Edited, designed and produced by
Eddison Sadd Editions Limited
St Chad's House, 148 King's Cross Road
London WC1X 9DH

Phototypeset by Wyvern Typesetting Limited,
Bristol, England in Fry's Baskerville and Baskerville No. 2
Origination by Columbia Offset, Hong Kong

Printed in Great Britain by
Bath Press Colourbooks, Blantyre, Glasgow

CONTENTS

ACKNOWLEDGMENTS
192

INTRODUCTION

Like any other besotted young mother, I wanted the very best for my babies. As a food lover and Cordon Bleu cook I wanted them to enjoy the wonderful tastes and aromas of fresh foods. With common sense, extensive research, two cooperative infants and a tolerant husband I knew I could create delicious recipes. Prepared quickly and easily they would be better for babies and toddlers than commercial gluten-free, vitamin- and iron-fortified powders and foods in jars.

The pleasure of seeing my children enjoy my foods has been a wonderful experience. I am reassured to know they are eating good fresh produce not over-processed convenience foods. Why should I feed my children from packets and jars when I would never give them to my husband or friends?

From six months babies have excellent taste buds and can appreciate a wide range of foods. This book will help you give your babies a healthy eating pattern for life. Instead of bland purées and oversweet desserts your children can enjoy a wide variety of tasty, wholesome dishes. Indeed, most of the recipes for toddlers can be enjoyed by the whole family.

All pediatricians and child nutritionists have their own theories and the more people you ask, the more muddled you become. No wonder mothers turn to commercial baby food. However, a report in April 1991 by The Food Commission found that as many as 40 percent of store-bought baby foods failed to meet with minimum nutrient levels that doctors have recommended. Added water and thickeners are used to bulk out small amounts of basic ingredients. There is also no indication on the labeling of baby foods as to the amount of each ingredient. Only 2 out of 22 meat-based baby foods provided more than 20 percent meat and some well known brands as little as 4 percent meat. Some 'low-sugar' rusks contained more sugar than a doughnut. Believe me, there is no mystique to feeding babies and toddlers and the benefit of home-cooked food is that you know exactly what ingredients your child is eating.

This book is for mothers who want their babies and toddlers to eat well and enjoy their food. The majority of recipes are easily made and do not need hours in the kitchen. The longer you spend cooking the more fractious you feel when your child refuses food. With a liquidizer or food processor and ice-cube trays, a month's supply can be prepared in one morning. Liquidize a variety of foods and freeze them as purée ice-cubes. Simply thaw them as needed for an instant, freshly prepared meal. If your baby won't eat, little time has been wasted so you will not feel too offended.

I give guidelines but there are no hard and fast rules to feeding a baby. Babies under one year should not have salt added to their food; salt in moderation after this will do no harm. Restricting salt intake may reduce the incidence of hypertension in later life. When possible I cook for the whole family and I believe most husbands would not appreciate unseasoned chicken, bland rutabaga and unsweetened apple betty.

If there are rules – and rules are made to be broken – they are to aim for:

1. Fresh food
2. Low animal fat
3. Low sugar
4. Low salt (No salt before one year)

A baby in the home is an opportunity to look at the dietary rules for the whole family. Some of these recipes are so delicious I serve them when entertaining! Babies' nutrition in their first year probably has greater influence than at any other time of life. This reinforces the need to start early with a good balanced diet. When your child opts for the raw fruits and vegetables, which adults imagine kids hate, over sugary candy you will recognise your success.

Good luck, I hope you and your child enjoy many happy meals together!

CHAPTER ONE

THE BEST FIRST FOODS FOR YOUR BABY

Many mothers feel that, once their baby is three months old, they should be starting to feed him solids. In fact there is no 'right' age as every baby is different.

Physiologically, there is no rush to get your baby started on solids. A baby's digestive system is not fully matured for the first few months and foreign proteins very early on may increase the likelihood of allergic food problems later. However, be warned, socially there is a kind of competitive spirit amongst mothers to get their child on to puréed steak and fries as soon as possible! I would advise that, provided your child is satisfied and growing properly, you should wait until he is between four and six months old before starting to give him simple solid foods.

Milk is Still the Major Food

It is very important to remember when starting your baby on solids that milk is still the most natural and the best food for growing babies. I would encourage mothers to try breast-feeding. Apart from the emotional benefits, breast milk contains antibodies that help protect infants from infection. In the first few months, they are particularly vulnerable and the colostrum a mother produces in the first few days of breast-feeding is a very important source of antibodies which help to build up a baby's immune system. (There are enormous benefits in breast-feeding your child even for as little as one week.) It is also medically proven that breast-fed babies are less likely to develop certain diseases in later life.

Milk should contain all the nutrients that your baby needs to grow. There are 65 calories in 4 fl oz (½ cup) of milk and formula milk is fortified with vitamins and, for babies over 4 months, also with iron. Cow's milk is not such a 'complete' food for human babies so is best not started until your baby is one year old.

Solids are introduced to add *bulk* to a baby's diet, and to introduce new tastes, textures and aromas; they also help the baby to practise using the muscles in his mouth. But giving a baby too much solid food too early may lead to constipation, and fewer nutrients than he needs. It would be very difficult for a baby to get the equivalent amount of nutrients from the small amount of solids as he gets from his milk.

Do not use softened water when making up your baby's bottle or repeatedly boiled water because of the danger of concentrating mineral salts. Babies' bottles should not be warmed in a microwave, as the milk may be too hot even though the bottle feels cool to the touch. Warm bottles standing in hot water.

There is no fixed rule as to how much milk a baby should consume during the day. However, it is important to make sure (especially as it is highly likely that a bottle may not be finished at each feed) that up to the age of five months, your baby drinks milk at least four times a day. If the number of feeds is reduced too quickly, your baby will not be able to drink as much as is needed. Some mothers make the mistake of giving their baby solid food when he or she is hungry, when what he really needs is an additional milk feed.

Although most babies of six months are perfectly able to drink pasteurised cow's milk and many mothers, especially in other countries, start their babies on cow's milk this early, it is best to continue with breast or formula milk for one year.

Dairy products like yogurt and cheese can be introduced after six months and are usually very popular with babies. Choose whole milk products rather than low-fat.

Fresh is Best

Fresh foods just *do* taste, smell and look better than jars of pre-prepared baby foods. Neither is there any doubt that, prepared correctly, they are better for your baby (and you), for it is inevitable nutrients, especially vitamins, are lost in the processing of pre-prepared baby foods. Home-made food tastes quite different from the jars you can buy. (If you were ever to try a blind tasting of popular brands of baby foods, you would know that it is very difficult to recognise what particular food each jar contains!)

There is also a very limited variety of single fruit and vegetables. Most of the jars available contain bland combinations of foods puréed to the same consistency so that it is difficult for your child to differentiate one food from another. It can be quite a problem getting your baby to accept the coarser texture of home-made purées once he is used to the very smooth texture of commercially prepared baby foods. It's best therefore to start cooking for your baby yourself right from the beginning. I believe your child is less likely to become a fussy eater if he is used to a wide selection of tastes and textures from a very early age. You can 'train' your child to enjoy the flavors of fresh spinach or apple and pea purée rather than crave candy and doughnuts. Why give them sugary and fatty foods when healthy food can be just as enjoyable?

Your Baby's Nutritional Requirements

The following six are essential nutrients that a child needs for a healthy diet and to promote growth.

PROTEINS

Proteins are needed for the growth and repair of our bodies, any extra can be used to provide energy (or is deposited as fat).

Proteins are made up of different amino acids. Some foods; meat, fish, dairy produce including cheeses, and soybeans, contain all the amino acids that are essential to our bodies. Other foods; grains, legumes, nuts and seeds, are still valuable sources of protein but do not contain all the essential amino acids.

CARBOHYDRATES

Carbohydrates and fat provide our bodies with their main source of energy. The former also provide fiber which adds bulk to our diet and acts as a natural laxative.

There are two types of carbohydrate:

sugar is one and starch (which in complex form provides fiber) is the other. In both types there are two forms – the natural and the refined. In both cases, it is the natural form which provides a more healthy alternative.

SUGARS
Natural
Fruit and Fruit juices
Vegetables
Vegetable juices
Refined
Sugars and honey
Sweetened cordials and sodas
Sweet gelatins
Jellies and other preserves
Cakes and cookies

STARCHES
Natural
Whole-grain breakfast cereals, flour, bread and pasta
Brown rice
Potatoes
Legumes, peas and lentils
Bananas and many other fruits and vegetables
Refined
Processed breakfast cereals (i.e. sugar-coated flakes)
White flour, breads and pasta
White rice
Sugary cookies
Cakes

FATS

Fats provide a concentrated source of energy. The body also needs to store some fat to prevent excessive loss of body heat. Thus a certain amount of fat is essential in everyone's diet. Foods that contain fats also contain the fat-soluble vitamins A, D, E and K. The problem is that many people eat too much fat and the wrong type of fat.

There are two types of fat – saturated, which mainly comes from animal sources, and unsaturated which comes from vegetable sources. It is the saturated fats which are the most harmful and which may lead to high cholesterol levels and coronary disease later in life.

It is important to give your baby whole milk for at least the first two years but try to reduce fats in cooking and use butter and margarine in moderation. Try to reduce saturated fats in your child's diet by cutting down on red meat, especially fatty meats like lamb; replace with more chicken and fish. This may in fact be a good time to review the whole family's eating habits, and to cut out all that butter on Daddy's toast in the morning!

VITAMINS

The possibility of vitamin deficiencies in the developed world should not be ignored. The children most at risk are those who follow a Vegan diet (i.e. no animal products at all) and those drinking cow's milk from the age of six months. Pediatricians recommend that these children should take a daily vitamin supplement until they are at least two.

For most children eating fresh food in sufficient quantity and drinking breast or formula milk until one year of age, vitamin supplements are unnecessary.

There are two types of vitamins – water-soluble (C and B complex) and fat-soluble (A, D, E and K). Water-soluble vitamins cannot be stored by the body so foods containing these should be eaten daily. They can also easily be destroyed by overcooking, especially when fruit and vegetables are boiled in water. You should try to preserve these vitamins by eating the foods raw or just lightly cooked (in a steamer, for instance).

There is some controversy over

FATS
Saturated
Butter
Meat
Lard, suet and drippings
Eggs
Cheese and full-fat yogurt
Cakes and cookies
Hard margarine
Whole milk
Unsaturated fats
Sunflower, grapeseed, safflower, sesame, soy, canola and olive oils
Soft polyunsaturated margarine
Oily fish (e.g. mackerel)

VITAMIN A

Essential for growth, healthy skin, tooth enamel and good vision.

Liver
Oily fish
Carrots
Dark green vegetables (e.g. broccoli)
Sweet potatoes
Oranges
Squash
Tomatoes
Lentils
Watercress
Apricots and peaches
Whole milk and eggs
Butter and margarine

VITAMIN B COMPLEX

Essential for growth, changing food into energy, for a healthy nervous system and as an aid to digestion. There are a large number of vitamins in the B group. Some are found in many foods, but no foods except for liver and yeast extract contain them all.

Meat, especially meat juices (so use in gravy) and liver
Fish
Dairy produce and eggs
Whole-grain cereals
Wheatgerm
Dark green vegetables
Potatoes
Yeast extract (e.g. Vegemite)
Nuts
Legumes
Bananas

VITAMIN C

Is needed for growth, healthy tissue and healing of wounds. It helps in the absorption of iron.

Vegetables such as: broccoli; Brussels sprouts; greens; bell peppers; potatoes; spinach; cauliflower.
Fruits such as: oranges and other citrus fruits; blueberries; melon; papaya; strawberries and tomatoes

VITAMIN D

Essential for proper bone formation, it works in conjunction with calcium. It is found in few foods, but is made by the skin in the presence of *sunlight*.

Oily fish
Liver
Oils
Eggs
Margarine
Dairy produce

VITAMIN E

Important for the composition of the cell structure, and helps the body to create and maintain red blood cells.

Vegetable oils
Margarine
Wheatgerm
Nuts

VITAMIN K

Aids in blood clotting, maintains bones, and is present in the intestine.
It is found in most vegetables and whole-grain cereals.

whether vitamin supplements can improve your child's IQ. As vitamins are necessary for the correct development of the brain and nervous system, it is important that a good supply of all vitamins is taken. However, a good balanced diet should supply all that is required and an excess of vitamins is potentially harmful. Good sources of all the major vitamins and minerals are given in the tables to the left.

CALCIUM

Calcium is needed for strong bones good teeth and growth.

Dairy produce, especially milk
Canned fish with bones (e.g. sardines, but only for older children)
Dried fruit
Bread and flour
Broccoli
Legumes

IRON

Iron is needed for healthy blood and muscles. A deficiency in iron is probably the most common and will leave your child feeling tired and run down.

Liver and red meat
Oily fish
Egg yolks
Dried fruits (especially apricots)
Whole-grain cereals
Lentils and legumes
Green leafy vegetables
Chocolate

WATER

Humans can survive for quite a time without food, but only a few days without water. Babies lose more water through their kidneys and skin than adults and also through vomiting and diarrhea.

Thus it is very important that your baby should not be allowed to dehydrate. Make sure he drinks plenty of fluids. Cool, boiled water is the best drink to give your baby on hot days particularly, as it will cool the body down quicker than any sugary drink.

It is really not necessary to give a very young baby anything to drink other than milk or plain water if he is just thirsty. Fruit sirups, cordials and other sweetened drinks should be discouraged to prevent dental decay. Don't be fooled if the packet says 'dextrose' – this is just a type of sugar.

If your baby refuses to drink water then give him unsweetened baby juice or fresh 100 percent fruit juices. Dilute according to instructions or for fresh juice use one part juice to three parts water, gradually increasing to half and half.

The Question of Allergies

It is fairly common for babies to inherit food allergies from their parents, and where there is a history of a particular food allergy, that food should only be introduced singly and with great care.

The commonest foods which carry a

risk of allergic reaction in babies are cow's milk and dairy products, eggs, fish (especially shellfish), some fruits, nuts and foods containing gluten. Some babies (and older children) can also react to artificial food colorings and additives. The commonest allergic problems which may be triggered by adverse reactions to food are: nausea; vomiting; diarrhea; asthma; eczema; hayfever; rashes and swelling of the eyes, lips and face. This is one reason it is unwise to rush starting your baby on solid foods.

There is no need to be unduly worried about food allergy, unless there is a family history. The incidence of food allergy in normal babies is extremely small and, with the tendency to a later introduction of solid food between four and six months, they have become even less common. However, it is still children under the age of eighteen months who are most likely to develop an allergy to a particular food. Although a lot of children 'grow out of it' by the age of two, some food allergies – particularly a sensitivity to eggs, milk, shellfish or nuts – can last for life. If your child has an allergy, do tell friend's mums and the school when he is old enough.

Never be afraid to take your baby to the doctor if you are worried that there is something wrong. Young babies' immune systems are not fully matured and babies can become ill very quickly if they are not treated properly and can develop serious complications.

LACTOSE INTOLERANCE

Lactose intolerance is not actually an allergy. Children who suffer lactose intolerance lack the substance lactase, an enzyme present in the superficial layers of the small bowel, which breaks lactose down to simpler sugars. Lactose is present in all milks and these babies will not be able to drink breast or cow's milk. A soy formula is given.

Some children who are lactose intolerant are able to eat dairy products like cheese and yogurt with no ill effects.

COW'S MILK PROTEIN ALLERGY

If your baby is sensitive to cow's milk, consult your doctor who will probably recommend a soy-based milk formula. Unmodified soy milk is not suitable as it is nutritionally inadequate. However, some babies who are allergic to cow's milk are also allergic to soy-based milks and for those babies there are a number of hypo-allergic milk formulas available on prescription. Breast milk is the best milk for babies who are allergic to cow's milk but mothers may need to limit dairy foods themselves as these can be transferred to their baby through breast milk.

No dairy products are tolerated in this condition and in the weaning diet milk-free vegetable or soy margarine may be substituted for butter and carob for milk chocolate. Very often babies outgrow this allergy by the age of two.

EGGS

Avoid giving egg whites before one year. Cooked egg yolks may be given once the baby is well established in mixed feeding, between eight and nine months.

FISH

Most pediatricians advise mothers not to give fish to their babies before eight months and to avoid all shellfish.

FRUITS

Some children can have an adverse reaction to citrus and berry fruits. Avoid these before 1 year but be sure to choose a Vitamin-C-rich drink.

NUTS

Nuts, even ground, should be avoided for at least the first seven months. Children under three can choke on whole nuts.

GLUTEN

If there is a family history of gluten intolerance babies under six months must follow a gluten-free diet but it is preferable for all young babies. Gluten is found in

wheat, rye, barley and oats and gluten sensitivity can cause celiac disease which, although rare can be serious.

When buying baby cereals and rusks, choose varieties that are gluten-free. Baby rice is the safest to try at first and thereafter there are plenty of alternate gluten-free products such as soy, cornstarch, rice, millet and potato flour for thickening and baking, brown rice, rice noodles, buckwheat spaghetti etc.

Preparing Baby Foods

Preparing and cooking baby foods is not difficult, but because you are dealing with a young baby, considerations like hygiene must be of the utmost importance.

EQUIPMENT

Most of the equipment needed will already be in your kitchen – mashers, graters, strainers etc – but the following three pieces I consider are vital!

Food mill A hand-turned food mill or ricer with variable cutting discs purées the food, separating it from the seeds and skin which can be difficult for the baby to digest. It is best used for fruit, vegetables, fish and the softer textured meats such as chicken and liver.

Blender or food processor This is useful for puréeing larger quantities. However, foods for young babies will often need to be pushed through a strainer afterwards to remove any seeds and skin.

Steamer The best way to preserve the fresh taste and vitamins in fruits and vegetables is to cook them in a steamer. It is worth buying a good multi-tiered steamer which will enable you to cook several different foods at the same time. (A colander over a saucepan along with a well-fitting lid, is a cheaper alternate.)

STERILIZING

At first, it is very important to sterilize bottles, and particularly, the teats that your baby sucks, properly by whatever approved method you choose. Warm milk is the perfect breeding ground for bacteria and if bottles are not properly washed and sterilized, your baby can become very ill. It is also best to sterilize the dishes and spoons you use for feeding your baby. It would be impossible, however, to sterilize *all* the equipment you use for cooking and puréeing baby food, but take extra care to keep everything very clean.

Use a dishwasher if you have one; the water is at a much higher temperature than it would be possible to use if washing the utensils by hand and helps to sterilize your equipment. However, once it is removed from the dishwasher, it does not remain sterile; bottles should be filled with milk immediately and stored in the fridge. Dry utensils with paper towels rather than a non-sterile dish towel.

Milk bottles should continue to be sterilized until your baby is one year old, but there is really not much point steriliz-ing spoons or food containers beyond the age when your baby crawls and puts everything in reach into his mouth.

COOKING BABY FOODS

Fruit and vegetables can lose nutrients when they are cooked so it makes sense to eat some both cooked and raw. However, raw ones would be difficult to digest for a young baby so, until the age of six months, most fruit and vegetables (apart from ripe bananas) should be cooked. As the baby gains teeth and learns to chew, the fruit or vegetables can be cooked more lightly in order to retain Vitamin C and crispness. After about six months, your baby can have purées of raw fruit and fresh grated fruit; raw or very *al dente* vegetables can be given as a finger food.

Cook in many ways – boiling, steaming, stewing or baking. Try to avoid fat-based methods of cooking such as frying (or cut down on the amount of fat used). Steaming, as mentioned above, is by far the best and, to maximize on nutritional benefits, the water in which or over which vegetables have cooked (so long as it does not contain salt) could be used as a drink or as the cooking water for something else such as pasta. Try also to maximize on fuel economy; steam a number of different foods at one time before puréeing and storing separately.

Cook fruit and vegetable purées for your baby by whichever method you choose. In each case make sure the purée is completely smooth, with no lumps. Later on you can adjust the texture of the purée to suit your baby as he starts to chew. Freeze any purée you are not using straightaway.

Boiling or steaming Wash fruit or vegetable carefully, peel, seed or pit as necessary and cut into small pieces. Add just enough water to cover and simmer until tender or steam (about 10 minutes, see individual recipes). Drain or remove from steamer, retaining the cooking water, then blend, mill or mash, adding some of the cooking water to bring it to the correct consistency for your baby.

Microwaving Peel, seed or pit the fruit or vegetable as necessary, and cut into slices. Put in a microwave dish with enough water just to cover and cover the dish with a lid. Microwave on High for about 3 minutes. Uncover, stir, re-cover and cook for another 2 minutes or until tender. Cooking times will vary according to how hard the fruit is to begin with. Blend, mash or mill to the right consistency, adding water as necessary.

FREEZING BABY FOODS

Whenever possible, prepare more food than is immediately needed and freeze the remainder in ice-cube trays for future meals. There are a limited number of foods that do not freeze well (like bananas and avocados) but most foods can be frozen with excellent results. Thus, in one or two hours a week, you can prepare enough to feed your baby for a month – making for a happier mother and baby and more time to spend together.

You will need a freezer which can freeze food to 0°F or below in 24 hours and sterile packaging. At the earliest stages, when only teaspoons of food are being taken, this means plastic ice-cube trays (sterilize these as well) and plastic freezer bags.

Cook and purée the food as described in the recipes, cover, leave to cool, then freeze until hard in ice-cube trays. Knock out and store in clearly labeled freezer bags. Label the food with the expiry date so you never give your baby food that is past its best.

FREEZER STORAGE TIMES	
Fruits	6 months
Vegetables	6 months
Purées with milk	4–6 weeks
Fish	10 weeks
Meat and chicken	10 weeks

Apple, pear, banana, papaya	4–5 months
Carrot, potato, zucchini, squash, green beans, rutabaga, sweet potato	4–5 months
Dried fruit, peach, kiwi, apricot, plum, melon, avocado	5–6 months
Peas, celery, bell pepper	5–6 months
Chicken, dairy products, broccoli, cauliflower, spinach, greens, leek	6 months
Other meats	6–12 months
Split pea, lima beans, lentils	8–9 months
Egg yolks	8–9 months
Fish	8–9 months
Citrus fruit, berries, tomato, mushrooms, honey, whole egg	1 year
Shellfish	over 2 years

To thaw one meal, remove the relevant number of cubes of food from the bag (only one at the very beginning) and leave at room temperature for an hour. Heat thoroughly, cool, then serve immediately. If using a microwave, stir well to make sure there is an even distribution of heat, allow to cool. Always test the temperature of food before giving it to your baby. Fruits to be served cold can thaw in the refrigerator overnight.

Never re-freeze foods which have already been frozen, and never reheat them more than once.

When can they have . . .?

I have listed below when you should introduce particular foods to your baby. This is not an exhaustive list and you should refer to each chapter for more information.

Meal Planners

In the next chapter I have devised some meal planners which will help you through the first weeks when you start to wean your baby. There are endless variations on the foods that can be given and the order in which they can be introduced.

If your baby's last meal is close to bed time, avoid giving him anything heavy or difficult to digest. This is certainly not the time to experiment with new foods if you both want a good night's sleep.

I have tried to give a wide choice of recipes, although I would expect that in practise meals that your baby enjoys would be repeated several times over the period of a week – and this is where your freezer will come in handy.

In each subsequent chapter, there are meal planners for your baby which you may follow or simply use as a guide. Adapt the charts according to what is in season and what you are preparing for your family. From nine months onwards, you should be able to cook for your baby and family together, perhaps eating the recipes you give your baby for lunch and supper for your own supper.

In these later charts, I have set out four meals a day. However, many babies are quite satisfied with three meals and some healthy snacks.

Many of the vegetable purées in the early chapters can be transformed into a vegetable soup; and a number of the vegetable dishes can serve as good side dishes for the family. If you give the baby some of the vegetables you are preparing for the family, make sure they have not been salted. In the later chapters many recipes are suitable for the whole family.

After each recipe you will find a symbol of two faces, one smiling, the other gloomy, each with a check box. You will find these useful in recording the success (or otherwise) of your baby meal recipes!

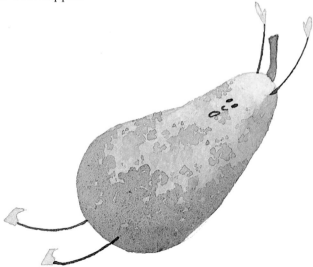

CHAPTER TWO

FOUR TO SIX MONTHS AND WEANING

In the recent past there was a lot of pressure on parents to start their babies on solid food much earlier than four months – this pressure was variously commercial, medical and social (keeping up with the neighbor's baby!). Ideas have now changed and this is all to the good, for many quite ordinary foods, as already discussed, can cause allergies. Neither is a baby's digestive system capable, until at least three months old, of absorbing foods more complex than baby milk.

When to Start Weaning

Every baby is different and some larger babies may just not be getting enough to satisfy them. Your baby will let you know when she needs to start solids; if, for example, she is no longer satisfied after a 8 fl oz bottle; if the interval between feeds becomes shorter over a prolonged period or if she starts becoming unsettled during the night. Another sure sign is when she reaches out and tries to chew everything in sight!

The First Solid Foods

'Solids' is a strange word to use for the mush we give to our babies and it is a little misleading.

Try only *one food at a time* at the very beginning. Offer apple purée for instance for a couple of days before giving her pear or banana. In that way, if there is a reaction, you will know what caused it. Later on, you can make it all more interesting by *combining* different foods.

The other vital point is that you *should not reduce the milk intake*. Milk is still the most important factor in her growth and development.

On pages 38–41 I have set out some feeding charts which will help you when you start to wean your baby. Use these charts as a guide, adapting them according to what is in season and what you are preparing for your family.

RICE

Initially I should advise one of the commercial baby rice cereals. These, although refined, are enriched with vitamins and they should also be free of sugar and salt. (This information will be printed on the box and in fact this is a good time to start reading the lists of contents of all boxes, jars and cans to look out for undesirables.) Baby rice is also easily digested. Make it up with baby milk or boiled cooled water according to the instructions on the box.

FRUIT

Since most babies are born with a 'sweet tooth' (breast milk is naturally sweet), you should have no trouble in getting your baby to enjoy eating fruit. Fruit that is fully ripe is naturally sweet. If you think a purée is sour-tasting, you can add a little sugar or some apple juice. Remember though, that the baby may actually prefer something less sweet than you and that is all to the good!

Most fruits provide Vitamin C and minerals and the yellow fruits contain Vitamin A. At first a baby should have cooked purées of fruits like apples and pears; ripe bananas are the only fruit that can be eaten raw at this stage. At about six months, your baby can graduate to raw mashed fruits; pears, papaya, melon, peaches, grapes and plums are all delicious as long as they are ripe.

Fresh fruits are best but fruits canned

in their own juice or water (*not* in a sirup) could also be used. Dried fruits should be introduced later and in small quantities; although they are nutritious they tend to be a laxative.

VEGETABLES

Some people prefer to start their babies on vegetables rather than fruit. Because most babies will take to eating fruit quite happily, they feel it is important to establish a liking for less sweet tastes.

Vegetables contain Vitamins A, C, E and K, as well as various minerals of value to a growing baby. Different vegetables provide different food values – green, Vitamin C, yellow, Vitamin A, for instance – so a variety is of value at later stages. At the beginning, though, when just introducing a baby to solids, it is best to start with root vegetables, particularly carrots, since they are naturally sweet.

Many vegetables have quite strong flavors – broccoli for instance – so when solids are fairly well established, you could mix in some potato to make it more palatable. Very young babies like their food quite bland.

Textures

At the very beginning of weaning, the rice and fruit or vegetable purées should be fairly wet and soft. This means that most vegetables, for instance, should be cooked until very soft so that they purée easily. You will probably need to thin out the consistency of the purées since babies are more likely to accept food in a semi-liquid form. You can use formula or breast milk, fruit juice or boiled water.

As your baby becomes more accustomed to the feel of 'solid food' in her mouth, you can gradually reduce the amount of liquid that you add to the purées, which will encourage her to chew a little. This should be a natural process as she should want to chew her food as she starts teething (usually between six and twelve months). You could also *thicken* the purées if necessary with baby rice or some crumbled rusk. As the baby becomes older and solid feeding is established (at the age of about six months), some fruit can be served raw and vegetables can be cooked more lightly (retaining more Vitamin C). Food can also be mashed or finely chopped to encourage chewing later on.

Remember to peel, core and seed fruits as necessary before cooking and/or puréeing (or put them through a food mill). Vegetables with fibers or seeds should be strained or put through a mill for a smooth texture. The husks of leguminous vegetables cannot be digested at this stage.

Quantities

At the very beginning, don't expect your baby to take more than 1–2 teaspoons of her baby rice or a fruit or vegetable purée. For this you should need 1 portion – in this section, this means a cube from an ice-cube tray. This is approximately 1 tablespoon in volume, but you'll need this much because of spitting and spills!

By the time your baby is six months, she could have graduated to eating 1–2 tablespoons of solids at each meal, which means *two* frozen food-cubes.

Drinks

Water, as outlined on page 13, is the best drink to offer. But freshly squeezed fruit and vegetable juices have a good nutritional value, being high in Vitamin C. A juicer is a useful appliance to have at home. Dilute fresh juices with an equal amount of cooled boiled water. (Never boil fruit juices or they lose their vitamin content.) Apple juice is not high in Vitamin C but is still a good drink and baby juices, available in a variety of flavors, including apple, are usually fortified with Vitamin C.

Over the next pages I give guidance on the preparation of different fruits and vegetables. They are not all suitable straight away so an indication of when they can be introduced is given on page 18.

TIPS FOR INTRODUCING SOLIDS

1 Make the rice or purée fairly wet and soft at first, using breast or formula milk, an unsweetened juice or cooking water. A handy tip is to mix the purée in the plastic removable top of a feeding bottle (which has been sterilized).

2 Hold your baby comfortably in the feeding position and relax. It would be better if *both* of you were protected against spills!

3 Choose a time when your baby is not frantically hungry and give her some milk first to partially satisfy her – she will then be more receptive to the new idea.

4 Babies are unable to lick food off a spoon with their tongues, so choose a small, *shallow* plastic teaspoon off which she can take some food with her lips. (Special feeding spoons can be bought.)

5 Start by giving just one solid feed during the day, about 1–2 teaspoons to begin with. I prefer to give this feed at lunchtime.

FRUIT AND VEGETABLES

Apple

Choose a sweet variety of dessert apple. Peel, halve, core and slice 2 medium apples. Put into a heavy saucepan with enough water to cover and cook over a low heat until soft (about 10 minutes). Or steam over water for the same length of time. Purée.

Apple and Cinnamon

Simmer 2 sweet apples, prepared as above, in apple juice to cover. Add a cinnamon stick. Cook as above, remove stick before puréeing.

MAKES 5 PORTIONS

Pear

Peel, halve and core 2 pears, then cut into small pieces. Cover with a little water, cook over a low heat until soft (about 8 minutes). Or steam over water for the same length of time. Purée.

When your baby is six months or older, there is no longer any need to cook the pear before making it into a purée, provided that the fruit is ripe.

MAKES 5 PORTIONS

Banana

This is the first uncooked fruit that a baby should be given. Use a very ripe banana. Use 1½ inches and mash very well with a fork to make it as smooth as possible. Add a little boiled water or baby milk if it is too thick and sticky for your baby to swallow.

If the banana is not ripe enough, split the skin and heat it in the oven or microwave for a couple of minutes to ripen before preparing.

Do not freeze bananas.

MAKES 1 PORTION

Papaya

Papaya is an excellent fruit to give a very young baby. It has a pleasing sweet taste which is not too strong and blends within seconds to a perfect texture. Ripe fruit has a yellowish skin.

Cut a medium fruit in half, remove all the black seeds and scoop out the flesh. Steam for 3–5 minutes, then purée.

When your baby is over six months, papaya may be eaten raw.

MAKES 4 PORTIONS

Cream of Fruit

Combining a fruit purée with baby milk and baby rice or crumbled rusk can make it more palatable for your baby. In the next few months, when your baby may start eating some other exotic fruits like mango and kiwi, this method of 'diluting' the fruit purées with milk will also make them less acidic.

Peel, core, steam or boil and purée the fruit of your choice as described. For 4 portions of prepared fruit, stir in 1 tablespoon unflavored baby rice or half a low-sugar rusk and 2 tablespoons baby milk.

MAKES 7 PORTIONS

Three-Fruit Purée

This is a delicious combination of three of the first fruits that your baby can eat.

Mix 2 teaspoons each of pear and apple purées (see page 24) with half a banana, mashed. Later (after six months), you can use half a raw ripe pear, peeled, cored and cut into chunks. Put this and the half banana through a food mill to make a smooth purée, then mix together with the 2 teaspoons of cooked apple purée.

MAKES 4 PORTIONS

Carrot

Small thin carrots are sweetest, so choose these if possible.

Peel, trim and slice 2 medium carrots. Either steam the carrot slices until tender (15 minutes), or boil in about ¾ cup boiling water (about 10 minutes). Purée in a food processor, blender or mill until the desired consistency. Add cooled boiled water, a teaspoon at a time to the steamed vegetable to make a smooth purée. Drain the boiled vegetable, reserving the cooking liquid and add as much of this as is necessary to make the desired consistency. (As the baby gets older, there should be no need to add any extra water.)

The cooking time is longer for small babies. Once your baby can chew, cut the time down to preserve Vitamin C and keep the vegetables crisper.

MAKES 4
PORTIONS

Rutabaga, Turnip and Parsnip

Use half a rutabaga, or ¾ cup of turnip or parsnip, scrubbed, peeled and cut into small cubes. Cover with ¾ cup boiling water and simmer, covered, until tender (about 20 minutes). Drain, reserving the cooking liquid and mash well with a fork.

MAKES 4
PORTIONS

Butternut Squash

Butternut squashes are the same shape as avocado pears. They have a hard peach-colored skin, orange flesh and a lovely sweet taste.

Peel and halve a small butternut squash, weighing about 4 oz. Remove seeds and cut the flesh into 1–inch cubes. Steam until tender (about 8 minutes). Transfer to a blender and process until a purée of the desired consistency.

MAKES 4 PORTIONS

Green Beans

Trim, remove any stringy bits and cut beans diagonally into thin slices to make 1 cup. Steam until tender (about 8–10 minutes), then put in a blender and process. Add a little boiled water or baby milk to make a smooth purée. Any variety of green bean is suitable but smaller, younger beans are more tender. Later on whole beans make great finger food with a sauce (see Green Fingers page 92).

MAKES 4 PORTIONS

Broccoli and Cauliflower

Use 1 cup of either, washed well and cut into small flowerets. Add a good ½ cup boiling water. Simmer, covered, until tender (about 10–15 minutes). Drain, reserving the cooking liquid. Put through a mill, adding a little of the reserved liquid (or baby milk) to make the purée the desired consistency.

Or steam the flowerets for 15 minutes for better flavor and retention of nutrients. Once your baby has teeth and can chew, cut the time down to 8–10 minutes to keep the vegetables crisp. Add boiled water or baby milk to make a smooth purée.

MAKES 4 PORTIONS

Zucchini

Wash 2 medium zucchini carefully, remove the ends and slice. (The skin is soft, so does not need to be removed.) Steam until tender (about 10–15 minutes), then put through a mill or mash with a fork. (No need to add extra liquid.)

MAKES 8 PORTIONS

Potato

Carefully wash a small (4 oz) potato, removing any blemishes from the skin, then cover with ½ cup boiling water and simmer until tender (about 20–30 minutes). Peel off the skin, then mash until smooth. Add enough baby milk to make the purée the desired consistency.

Alternately, bake a potato in the oven preheated to 400°F for about 1 hour or until soft. Scoop out the inside and mash with a little baby milk. (Later on, keep the baked potato skins, as they are very good for babies to chew on when teething.)

Save fuel and time by cooking these with the family meal or cook many more portions. Small quantities are most economically cooked in the microwave.

MAKES 5 PORTIONS

Cream of Carrot Purée

A creamy purée with milk and baby rice can be made with many different vegetables. Make a purée with ½ cup of cubed carrot (page 25). Mix 2–3 teaspoons unflavored baby rice with ¾ cup warm baby milk. Vary the amount of rice according to how thick you want the purée. Stir the baby rice mixture into the vegetable purée. Half a low-sugar rusk mixed with a similar quantity of baby milk will also make a creamy purée. Allow the rusk to soften in the baby milk before mixing it into the vegetable purée of your choice.

MAKES 12 PORTIONS

Potato, Zucchini and Green Beans

Combining potato with green vegetables makes them more palatable for your baby. Peel and chop a medium potato. Boil in water below a steamer for 35 minutes until soft. Steam ¼ cup trimmed and sliced green beans with 1 trimmed and sliced zucchini above the potato for the last 10 minutes of cooking time. Drain the potato and purée with the other vegetables in a mill.

MAKES 7 PORTIONS

Peas with a Hint of Mint

Mint perks up the flavor of this recipe but you can leave it out if your baby prefers. Put ⅔ cup shelled peas and ½ cup trimmed green beans with a small sprig of mint in a saucepan and cover with 1 cup of water. Simmer for 10 minutes, remove the mint sprig and purée the vegetables in a food mill to get rid of the indigestible husks from the peas.

Apart from being a well-suited flavoring for peas and beans, mint is a well known carminative. A weak infusion of mint leaves can help to relieve painful gas and colic for your baby.

MAKES 4 PORTIONS

Peach

Bring a small saucepan of water to a boil. Cut a shallow cross on the skin of 2 peaches, submerge them in the water for 1 minute, then plunge into cold water. Skin the peaches, and chop, discarding the pits. Steam the peaches until tender (about 5 minutes), purée.

Prepare fresh apricots in the same way. Both can be eaten raw, if ripe, after six months.

MAKES 4 PORTIONS

Carrot and Celery Purée

Combining vegetables makes them more interesting and once your baby has got used to carrot and celery purée separately, this combination makes a nice change. Cook ½ cup carrots, scraped and sliced, in boiling water for 20 minutes until soft. After 10 minutes, add 1 cup chopped celery. Drain the vegetables and purée in a mill. Stir in 2 tablespoons baby milk.

MAKES 8 PORTIONS

Cantaloupe Melon

Cantaloupes are so sweet, fragrant and plentiful it is almost a bonus that they are rich in Vitamins A and C. Cut in half, remove seeds and scoop out the flesh. Steam for 3–5 minutes, then purée.

Other varieties of sweet melon, so long as they are ripe, can be used too. To be genuinely sweet the melon needs to ripen on the vine. A truly ripe melon smells very fragrant; the stem end is slightly sunken and calloused, and yields to the touch. When your baby is over six months, properly ripe melon may be eaten raw.

MAKES 12–16 PORTIONS

Plum

Skin 2 large ripe plums as for peaches. Cut into pieces and bring to a boil in just enough water to cover. Simmer for about 5 minutes or until soft; add a little sugar to taste if the fruit is a little sour. (Alternately, steam for about 6 minutes.) Purée, adding as much of the cooking liquid as is necessary to make the desired consistency.

Plums may be eaten raw once your baby is over six months.

MAKES 4 PORTIONS

Prune and Dried Apricot

Use ⅔–¾ cup of fruit. Soak prunes in cold water overnight, then drain. Wash dried apricots well to remove preservative. Cover with fresh cold water, bring to a boil and simmer until soft (about 10 minutes). Drain, remove the pits and pass through a mill to remove skins. Add a little of the cooking liquid to make a smooth purée.

Prunes are excellent if your baby gets constipated.

MAKES 4 PORTIONS

Apricots and Pears

Fresh apricots have a very limited season but when they are available you should make this delicious combination of fruits. Apricots are rich in Vitamins A and C. Halve and pit 5 fresh ripe apricots. Peel, core and slice 2 ripe pears. Steam the fruit until tender, about 6–8 minutes. When cool enough skin the apricots. Purée the fruit together in a mill or blender

MAKES 12 PORTIONS

Semolina with Apples and Raisins

Semolina with milk has a very smooth texture and makes wonderful baby purées mixed with fruit for natural sweetness. Put 1 tablespoon semolina in a saucepan and stir in ⅜ cup milk over a gentle heat, add 6 raisins and a pinch of cinnamon and cook for 2 to 3 minutes. Put this mixture through a mill and stir in 1 tablespoon apple purée.

MAKES 2 PORTIONS

Fresh Peas

Cover 1 cup shelled peas with water, bring to a boil and simmer, covered, until tender (about 10 minutes). Drain, reserving some of the cooking liquid. Put the peas through a mill or a strainer and add a little of the cooking liquid to make the purée the desired consistency.

MAKES 4 PORTIONS

Tomatoes

Plunge 2 medium tomatoes in boiling water for 30 seconds, then transfer to cold water. Skin, remove the seeds and cook the flesh in a heavy-bottomed saucepan, mashing over a low heat for about 2 minutes. Put through a mill or strainer to purée.

MAKES 2–3 PORTIONS

Spinach

Use 2 cups chopped spinach leaves, washed very carefully and coarse stalks removed. Cover with boiling water and simmer, covered, until tender (about 10 minutes). Firmly press out all the excess water and put the cooked spinach leaves through a mill to purée.

MAKES 2 PORTIONS

Celery

Wash celery carefully, trim, and remove as many strings as possible. Cut into small pieces to make almost 1 cup, cover with boiling water and simmer until tender (about 15 minutes). Drain and put the celery through a mill to purée to a smooth consistency.

Shredded cabbage can be cooked similarly but for about 10 minutes only.

MAKES 4 PORTIONS

Red Bell Pepper

Wash a medium pepper, remove the core and seeds and cut the flesh into small cubes. Cover with boiling water and simmer, covered, for about 5 minutes. Drain and put through a food mill to get rid of the tough outer skin.

MAKES 2–3 PORTIONS

Avocado

Choose a well-ripened avocado, cut it in half and scoop out the pit. Use 1/3–1/2 and mash the flesh very carefully with a fork, making sure there are no lumps. Serve quickly, otherwise it will turn brown.

Do not freeze avocados.

MAKES 1 PORTION

Kiwi and Banana

Kiwi fruit are very good for your baby as they have more Vitamin C than an orange! Make sure you choose a very ripe fruit, otherwise it can be very sour.

MAKES 1 PORTION

¹/₄ ripe kiwi, peeled   *¹/₄ ripe banana, peeled*

Purée the kiwi and press through a fine strainer to get rid of the black seeds. Purée the banana and mix it with the kiwi. Eat straightaway or the banana turns brown.

Apple and Banana with Apple Juice

This makes a nice change from plain mashed banana or apple purée. When your baby is six months or older, you can make this with raw grated apple and mashed banana.

MAKES 1 PORTION

¹/₄ apple, peeled, cored and chopped   *¹/₂ teaspoon apple juice*
¹/₄ banana, peeled and chopped

Steam the apple until tender (about 10 minutes) then purée or mash it together with the banana and apple juice. Serve as soon as possible.

Peaches, Apples and Pears

This is a good purée to make when peaches are in season. When they are not it tastes good just with apples and pears.

MAKES 14 PORTIONS

2 dessert apples, peeled, cored and chopped
½-inch vanilla bean (optional)

2 ripe peaches, skinned and chopped
2 ripe pears, peeled, cored and chopped

Put the apple pieces in a saucepan with ¼ cup water and the vanilla bean. Simmer for about 5 minutes. Add the peaches and pears and cook for 5 minutes more. Remove the bean and purée.

Mixed Dried Fruit Compote

Dried fruits and fresh fruits are delicious combined. Later on mix with a little plain yogurt or cottage cheese.

MAKES 18 PORTIONS

½ cup each of dried apricots, dried peaches and prunes

1 dessert apple and pear, peeled, cored and chopped or 1 apple and 3 fresh apricots, skinned, pitted and chopped

Put the dried fruit into a saucepan, cover with plenty of boiling water and simmer for 25 minutes until tender. Add the apple and pear or apricots to the saucepan. Continue to simmer for another 10–15 minutes, adding more water if necessary. Purée in a mill.

Vegetable Broth

Vegetable broth forms the basis of many vegetable recipes. It is well worth making your own supply which will be free from additives and salt. Freeze it as you would any other broth.

MAKES ABOUT 4 CUPS

½ onion, peeled
1 carrot, scrubbed
1 celery stalk
1½ cups mixed root vegetables (rutabaga, turnip, parsnip, etc), peeled

1 bouquet garni (bought or home-made)
1 sprig of fresh parsley
1 bay leaf
a few black peppercorns

Chop all the vegetables, place in a pan and cover with water. Add the seasonings, bring to a boil and simmer for about 1 hour. Strain off and discard the vegetables and use the flavored water as broth.

☺ ☹

Zucchini and Banana Purée

This may seem a strange combination but they complement each other well.

MAKES 2 PORTIONS

1 small zucchini, washed, trimmed and sliced

½ small banana, peeled and sliced

Steam the zucchini slices for 8 minutes and purée in a food mill with the banana.

☺ ☹

Baby Cereal and Vegetables

Sometimes vegetable purées can be very watery – particularly those made from, say, zucchini which have a high water content. In this recipe I have added baby rice which makes an excellent thickening agent.

MAKES 16 PORTIONS

¹/₄ small onion, peeled
2 zucchini, trimmed
¹/₂ cup cubed rutabaga
2 medium carrots, peeled

¹/₄ cup shredded green cabbage
¹/₄ cup fresh peas
vegetable broth (see page 33)
3 tablespoons baby rice

Chop all the vegetables, put them in a saucepan and just cover them with the broth. Bring to a boil, then simmer for 30 minutes or until the vegetables are tender. Add the baby cereal and stir over a gentle heat for 2 minutes. Purée the vegetables in a blender until the desired consistency.

☺ ☹

Vegetable Medley

This is a good combination of fresh vegetables. Steamed beans, celery and zucchini also make great finger foods for slightly older babies. Do not steam the vegetables too long or they will become mushy and lose Vitamin C.

MAKES 10 PORTIONS

¹/₂ cup green beans, trimmed and sliced
¹/₂ cup sliced celery

¹/₂ cup zucchini, trimmed and sliced
¹/₄ small red bell pepper, skinned, seeded and chopped

Steam the beans, celery and zucchini for about 6–7 minutes. Add the pepper to the steamer and continue to cook until all the vegetables are tender (about another 4 minutes). Purée and strain the vegetables or put them through a mill.

Zucchini, Watercress and Potato Purée

Watercress is rich in calcium and iron. It blends well with the other vegetables to make a tasty, bright green purée. You can add a little milk if your baby prefers it that way.

MAKES 12 PORTIONS

a handful of watercress
1 large potato, peeled and chopped
1½ cups vegetable broth (see page 33)

2 teaspoons chopped parsley
1 medium zucchini, washed, trimmed and sliced
baby milk (optional)

Remove the leaves from the watercress and chop them into pieces. (Discard the stalks, or use them in making vegetable broth.) Put the leaves and the potato into the broth, bring to a boil and simmer for about 10 minutes. Add the parsley and zucchini and simmer for another 10 minutes. Purée the mixture in a mill and, if you like, add a little baby milk to adjust the consistency.

Avocado and Papaya

This is very simple to make and the two fruits blend very well.

MAKES 1 PORTION

¹/₄ small avacado   *¹/₄ small papaya*

Remove the flesh from the avocado and papaya and mash them together until smooth. This should be eaten soon after it is made or the avocado will turn brown.

Sweet Potato with Cinnamon

The addition of cinnamon gives the sweet potato an extra sweetness which babies love. This is very simple to make.

MAKES 7 PORTIONS

1 sweet potato (about 6 oz), peeled   *1 tablespoon baby milk*
and cut into chunks   *¹/₄ teaspoon powdered cinnamon*

Cover the sweet potato chunks with water, bring to a boil and simmer for about 30 minutes or until soft. Drain and mash together with the baby milk and cinnamon.

Carrot, Potato and Celery Purée

Adding baby milk to vegetables can make them more palatable for
your baby.

MAKES 4 PORTIONS

*¼ cup carrot, washed, scrubbed and
chopped into pieces*
*¼ cup celery, washed, trimmed and
chopped into pieces*

*1 small potato, peeled and cut into
pieces*
¼ cup baby milk

Put the vegetables in a saucepan and cover with 1 cup water.
Simmer for 15 minutes. Add the milk and make into a smooth
purée in a blender.

Baked Butternut Squash

The flavor of butternut squash is delicious simply baked with a
little apple juice, margarine and brown sugar. You can also scoop
out the seeds and stuff the squash with vegetables as in this recipe.

MAKES 6 PORTIONS

1 small butternut squash
1 teaspoon brown sugar
1 tablespoon apple juice

1 tablespoon margarine
1 small zucchini, diced
*¼ small red bell pepper, skinned,
seeded and diced*

Cut the squash in half lengthwise and scoop out the seeds. Mix the
rest of the ingredients together and divide between the two cavi-
ties. Cover both halves with foil and bake in the oven preheated to
350°F for 1½ hours. Scoop out the flesh and filling and purée.

FOUR TO FIVE MONTH MEAL PLANNER

Week 1	Breakfast	Sleep	Lunch	Sleep	Dinner	Bedtime
Days 1–7	Breast/bottle	Breast/bottle	Breast/bottle Baby rice	Breast/bottle	Diluted fruit juice	Breast/bottle
Week 2						
Day 1	Breast/bottle Baby rice	Breast/bottle	Breast/bottle	Breast/bottle	Diluted fruit juice Carrot	Breast/bottle
Day 2	Breast/bottle Baby rice	Breast/bottle	Breast/bottle	Breast/bottle	Diluted fruit juice Carrot	Breast/bottle
Day 3	Breast/bottle Baby rice Apple	Breast/bottle	Breast/bottle	Breast/bottle	Diluted fruit juice Carrot	Breast/bottle
Day 4	Breast/bottle Apple	Breast/bottle	Breast/bottle	Breast/bottle	Diluted fruit juice Rutabaga	Breast/bottle
Day 5	Breast/bottle Apple	Breast/bottle	Breast/bottle	Breast/bottle	Diluted fruit juice Rutabaga	Breast/bottle
Day 6	Breast/bottle Baby rice Pear	Breast/bottle	Breast/bottle	Breast/bottle	Diluted fruit juice Potato	Breast/bottle
Day 7	Breast/bottle Pear	Breast/bottle	Breast/bottle	Breast/bottle	Diluted fruit juice Potato	Breast/bottle

Fruit juice should be diluted at least 50/50 with cooled boiled water.

FOUR TO FIVE MONTH MEAL PLANNER

Week 3	Breakfast	Sleep	Lunch	Sleep	Dinner	Bedtime
Day 1	Breast/bottle Mashed banana	Breast/bottle	Breast/bottle	Breast/bottle	Diluted fruit juice Potato and green beans	Breast/bottle
Day 2	Breast/bottle Mashed banana	Breast/bottle	Breast/bottle	Breast/bottle	Diluted fruit juice Potato and green beans	Breast/bottle
Day 3	Breast/bottle Cream of Fruit	Breast/bottle	Breast/bottle	Breast/bottle	Diluted fruit juice Butternut squash	Breast/bottle
Day 4	Breast/bottle Cream of Fruit	Breast/bottle	Breast/bottle	Breast/bottle	Diluted fruit juice Butternut squash	Breast/bottle
Day 5	Breast/bottle Banana Papaya	Breast/bottle	Breast/bottle	Breast/bottle	Diluted fruit juice Green beans Baby rice	Breast/bottle
Day 6	Breast/bottle Pear	Breast/bottle	Breast/bottle	Breast/bottle	Diluted fruit juice Green beans Baby rice	Breast/bottle
Day 7	Breast/bottle Pear	Breast/bottle	Breast/bottle	Breast/bottle	Diluted fruit juice Carrot and Celery Purée	Breast/bottle

Fruit juice should be diluted at least 50/50 with cooled boiled water.

FOUR TO FIVE MONTH MEAL PLANNER

Week 4	Breakfast	Sleep	Lunch	Sleep	Dinner	Bedtime
Day 1	Breast/bottle Cream of Fruit	Breast/bottle	Breast/bottle	Breast/bottle	Fruit juice Cream of Carrot Purée	Breast/bottle
Day 2	Breast/bottle Cream of Fruit	Breast/bottle	Breast/bottle	Breast/bottle	Fruit juice Cream of Carrot Purée	Breast/bottle
Day 3	Breast/bottle Three Fruit Purée	Breast/bottle	Breast/bottle	Breast/bottle	Fruit juice Potato, Zucchini and Green Beans	Breast/bottle
Day 4	Breast/bottle Three Fruit Purée	Breast/bottle	Breast/bottle	Breast/bottle	Fruit juice Potato, Zucchini and Green Beans	Breast/bottle
Day 5	Breast/bottle mashed banana	Breast/bottle	Breast/bottle	Breast/bottle	Fruit juice Peas with a Hint of Mint	Breast/bottle
Day 6	Breast/bottle Apples and Cinnamon	Breast/bottle	Breast/bottle	Breast/bottle	Fruit juice Peas with a Hint of Mint	Breast/bottle
Day 7	Breast/bottle Apples and Cinnamon	Breast/bottle	Breast/bottle	Breast/bottle	Fruit juice Rutabaga	Breast/bottle

Fruit juice should be diluted at least 50/50 with cooled boiled water.

FIVE TO SIX MONTH MEAL PLANNER

	Breakfast	Sleep	Lunch	Sleep	Dinner	Bedtime
Day 1	Milk Baby cereal mixed fruit purée and milk	Milk	Carrot, Potato and Celery Purée Juice	Milk	Mashed banana Rusk Water or juice	Milk
Day 2	Milk Semolina with Apple and Raisins	Milk	Avocado Juice	Milk	Mixed Dried Fruit Compote Water or juice	Milk
Day 3	Milk Baby cereal Peach or pear	Milk	Sweet Potato with Cinnamon Juice	Milk	Cream of Fruit Water or juice	Milk
Day 4	Milk Dried apricot Baby cereal	Milk	Baby Cereal and Vegetables Juice	Milk	Papaya Rusk Water or juice	Milk
Day 5	Milk Baby cereal Papaya	Milk	Baked Butter- nut Squash Mashed banana Juice	Milk	Avocado and Papaya Rice cake Water or juice	Milk
Day 6	Milk Baby cereal Apple and Cinnamon	Milk	Potato, Zucchini and Green Beans Juice	Milk	Three-Fruit Purée Rusk Water or juice	Milk
Day 7	Milk Mixed Dried Fruit Compote Baby cereal	Milk	Zucchini, Watercress and Potato Purée Juice	Milk	Mashed banana Rice cake Water or juice	Milk

Fruit juice should be diluted at least 50/50 with cooled boiled water.

CHAPTER THREE

SIX TO NINE MONTHS

Between six and nine months is a rapid development period for your baby. A six-month old baby still needs to be held while you are feeding him and more often than not, still has no teeth. A nine-month old baby, however, is usually strong enough to sit in a high chair while he is being fed and has already cut a few teeth. Babies of eight months are usually quite good at holding food themselves and enjoy eating small finger foods like pieces of raw or cooked vegetables, pasta or raw fruits. (Turn to pages 72–78 for suitable finger foods for young babies.) Chewing on a piece of apple will help to relieve sore gums but *never* leave your baby unattended when eating; babies have a habit of chewing up a lot of food and storing it in their mouths without swallowing and they can very easily choke. A handy tip is to give your baby some dried apple to suck; it is easy for them to hold because of the hole in the middle; it is tough to chew on so they cannot bite pieces off; and it has a lovely sweet taste.

Less Milk, More Appetite

Once your baby is six months old, you can start cutting down on his milk feeds so that he is more hungry for his solids. However he should still be taking about 20 fl oz of milk per day, either as milk or in the dairy products he eats. You can offer plain water or fruit juices instead of milk to drink.

At eight or nine months, when your baby holds toys fairly well himself, he is probably ready to try drinking from a cup. First try a cup with a spout then remove the top and see how he manages with it open. A cup with a weighted base is good so that it does not topple over and spill when your baby puts it down. Lids that seal are good for traveling.

Let your baby's appetite determine how much he eats and never force him to eat something he actually dislikes. Do not offer it for a while, but re-introduce it a few weeks later. You may find that second time around he loves it.

Remember at this age it is quite normal for babies to be quite fat. As soon as your baby starts crawling and walking, he will lose this excess weight.

The Foods to Choose

Your baby can now eat protein foods like eggs, cheese, legumes, chicken and, after eight months, fish. Limit some foods which might be indigestible for your baby – spinach, lentils or cheese, and do not worry if some foods like legumes, peas and raisins pass through your child undigested; babies cannot completely digest husked vegetables and the skins of fruits until about two years old. Peeling, mashing and puréeing fruit and vegetables will of course aid digestion. With foods like bread, flour, pasta and rice, try to choose whole-grain (rather than refined) as it is more nutritious.

Once your baby has passed the six-month stage and is happily eating slightly coarser-textured foods, there is no need to continue giving your baby special baby cereals. You can use adult cereals like instant oatmeal, Grahams, and Chex which are just as nutritious and much cheaper. Choose a cereal which is not highly refined and is low in sugar and salt. Many people use commercial baby foods because they are easy to prepare; they also think, due to the long list of vitamins and minerals on the box, that they are more nutritious. However, babies who eat a good balanced diet of fresh foods get a perfectly adequate quantity of vitamins and minerals. Also baby foods in general are heavily processed and their finer texture and bland flavors hinder the development of your baby's tastes.

Beware, too, of some of the rusks you can buy which are supposedly the 'ideal food for your baby'. They are full of sugar (the amount often not even stated on the list of ingredients). Give your baby some toast to chew on or follow the simple recipe for rusks in the nine to twelve month finger-food section (see page 77).

Many of your own favorite recipes can be adapted for your baby once he is eight months old. When preparing a family dish, put aside the baby's portion before you add seasoning or spices and he can very often enjoy the same meal as everyone else. Many of the recipes from the previous age group's section can still be used – simply alter the texture slightly if appropriate and offer more.

You can now safely cook with cow's milk. This is not suitable for milk feeds (formula or breast is better).

FRUIT

There are few babies I know who do not like fruit. In the next few months, try to introduce your child to as wide a range of fruits as possible. Make fresh fruit salads with seasonal fruits chopped into little pieces and mixed with fruit juice. You will find which fruits your child likes best by seeing what he leaves.

Dried fruits and some exotic fruits like mango can give your child an upset stomach. Limit these or you may run out of diapers! Citrus and berry fruits should not be given in any quantity to babies under one year of age.

Fresh fruit makes excellent snacks – much better than processed, additive-laden, sugary foods which ruin developing teeth and upset a balanced diet.

VEGETABLES

Once your baby starts to get teeth, you will find that he enjoys chewing on slightly harder vegetables. Cut down the steaming time to preserve Vitamin C and keep them crisp. Cauliflower and broccoli flowerets, baby carrots and baby corn-cobs, for instance – make excellent finger foods. Give them to your baby with his favorite vegetable purée as a dip.

Remember that some vegetables such as new potatoes and zucchini should not be peeled to preserve nutrients in the skin. Combinations of fruit and vegetables are popular – try squash and apple; spinach and pear or devise your own.

FISH

Many children grow up disliking fish, which is a great shame as it is such a healthful food, full of protein and very low in fat. It's excellent for babies, easy to chew and digest and quick to cook.

I think one of the main reasons children are put off fish is that they find it bland and boring. Counteract this with stronger tastes like cheese or herbs. If your child gets excited at the prospect of fish for supper, then you deserve to be a very proud mum indeed.

Most pediatricians advise against fish before eight months. Start with white fish only and give oily fish after 10–12 months.

Be careful not to overcook fish, as it becomes tough and tasteless. It is cooked when the fish just flakes with a fork but is still firm. Always check very carefully for bones before serving fish.

MEAT

Chicken is the first meat that should be introduced to babies. Chicken is a great family favorite of ours; it is very versatile and I am always concocting new ways of serving it. I was keen to get Nicholas and Lara to like chicken from an early age so I could cook for the whole family.

I have found that babies like the mild taste of chicken. It is easy and quick to cook; a great help to busy mothers. Chicken blends very well with many vegetables and can have a smooth texture when puréed. Once your baby is able to handle food himself and has a few teeth, small pieces of chicken make excellent finger food and are softer and easier to chew than red meat chunks.

Home-made chicken broth forms the basis of many recipes and I recommend that you make it in large batches. Freeze in small containers or ice-cube trays.

PASTA

You will find that pasta is a great favorite with babies and mums as it is easy to chew, fun to eat and easy to cook.

For babies around six months, there are very tiny pasta shapes available which are sometimes used in soups and need no chewing or you could chop up spaghetti. Many of the vegetable purées make excellent pasta sauces, and you can always add a little grated cheese. Serve about $1/3$–$1/2$ cup cooked ($1/8$–$1/4$ cup dry) small pasta shapes per portion.

Textures

For babies between six and eight months, the recipes should be puréed to a fairly smooth consistency. Thereafter the mixture can be coarser, with the foods mashed, minced or grated or make a gradual transition by adding grated food to a purée. Foods must be soft enough for the toothless gums to chew.

Quantities

The portions quoted for each recipe are still ice-cube-tray size. Babies at this stage can eat between 1 and 4 tablespoons at each meal. On average thaw 4 frozen food-cubes, two for a 'main course' and two of a fruit purée for 'dessert'.

FRUIT

Baked Bananas

Babies love bananas and this recipe is scrumptious. For older children, you can make this recipe Jamaican style by using brown sugar instead of maple sirup and adding the juice of one orange. It can also be cooked in a frying pan and flambéed with rum for an adult dinner party. Serve with vanilla ice cream.

MAKES 1 PORTION

1 banana, sliced in half lengthwise   *powdered cinnamon*
1 teaspoon maple sirup   *margarine or butter*

Put the banana into an ovenproof dish. Pour over the maple sirup, sprinkle with a little cinnamon and dot with a little margarine or butter. Cover with foil and bake at 350°F for 10 minutes.

Avocado, Banana and Yogurt

This should be eaten straightaway before it turns brown.

MAKES 1 PORTION

2 slices avocado,   *1 tablespoon plain full-fat yogurt*
½ small banana, peeled

Scoop the flesh of the avocado from the skin and mash it together with the rest of the ingredients.

Apple and Baby Cereal

Try using different fruits such as peaches, mangos, plums and combinations like apple and raisin, and peach and cranberry.

MAKES 6 PORTIONS

1 dessert apple, peeled, cored and cut
into small pieces
⅓ cup natural apple juice

2 teaspoons baby cereal
2 teaspoons plain yogurt

Cook the apple over a low heat with the apple juice and 2 tablespoons water until soft (about 15 minutes). Purée the apple with the cooking liquid, then stir in the cereal and yogurt.

Peaches and Rice

You could use nectarines or plums or add raisins and spices.

MAKES 10 PORTIONS

¼ cup brown rice
apple juice

2 ripe peaches, skinned and pitted
plain yogurt or ricotta

Cover rice with apple juice and cook for 20 minutes or until tender. Purée the peaches, mix with the rice and bake in a buttered dish for 15–20 minutes at 350°F. Purée in a blender and serve plain or mixed with a little ricotta or yogurt.

Apple and Prunes with Sauce

MAKES 20 PORTIONS

8 prunes, soaked overnight
4 apples

Vanilla sauce
⅞ cup milk
1-inch vanilla bean
1 tablespoon cornstarch
1 teaspoon superfine sugar

Simmer the prunes gently in the soaking water till tender (about 10 minutes). Meanwhile make an apple purée (see page 24). Pit, then purée the prunes in a mill. Mix together with the apple purée.

To make the sauce, put ¾ cup milk in a saucepan with the vanilla bean and bring to a boil. Stir the cornstarch and sugar into the remaining cold milk and stir until smooth. Stir this into the hot milk off the heat. Bring to a boil and stir until thickened. Remove bean.

Cottage Cheese and Sharon Fruit

Sharon fruit is a variety of persimmon from Israel. It must be very ripe and soft before it is eaten, and tastes a little like a sweet plum. The second portion will keep in the fridge for the next day.

MAKES 2 PORTIONS

1 Sharon fruit, or 2 slices of mango
or papaya

2 tablespoons plain cottage cheese

Cut the Sharon fruit in half and remove the skin. Blend the flesh together with the cottage cheese until smooth.

Home-Made Fruit Gelatin

It is very easy to make fruit gelatin at home and it is not full of sugar or artificial colorings like some of the commercially prepared fruit gelatins. If you are short of time or don't have fresh fruit purées or juices to hand, flavored gelatin can be used for any of these recipes. Gelatin, of course, does not freeze but any extras have never been a problem in my house!

MAKES 12 PORTIONS

1 envelope of powdered gelatine   *2¹/₂ cups fresh fruit juice or fruit purée*

Sprinkle the gelatin over ¹/₄ cup warmed fruit juice (or water if using fruit purée) in a cup. Stand the cup in a pan of hot water if necessary until gelatin dissolves. Pour into the remaining fruit juice or purée, stirring thoroughly. Pour into a suitable container, cool, then chill until set.

<u>Fruit Gelatin Shapes</u> Set gelatin in an 8-inch square pan, lined with foil. Turn the pan over, remove the foil and make different shapes from the gelatin using cookie cutters.

<u>Fruit and Yogurt Gelatin</u> Make up ¹/₂ quantity of any fruit flavored gelatin and chill for 30 minutes, then stir in a complementary flavored fruit yogurt. Chill again to set. This gelatin will not set firm and so is not suitable for a mold.

<u>Stop Light Gelatin</u> Make up a ¹/₂ quantity of gelatin using a green colored fruit juice or purée. Pour into a large fluted gelatin mold. (A wet mold makes it easier to turn the gelatin out.) Chill for 1¹/₂ hours. Repeat with an orange colored juice or purée and pour on top. Chill again and then add a layer of a red gelatin. Chill until set. Dip into hot water, cover with a plate and then turn over to unmold.

VEGETABLES

Lentil Purée

Lentils are usually soaked overnight but you can take a shortcut.
Rinse them, cover generously with the broth, bring to a boil and
boil for 2 minutes. Take off the heat, cover the pan and let the
lentils absorb the broth for 1–2 hours.
Lentils are a good cheap source of protein but are best not given
to babies before eight months.

MAKES 36 PORTIONS

¹/₄ cup split red lentils
2¹/₂ cups chicken broth (preferably
home-made, see page 62)
1 carrot

1 potato
¹/₂ small onion
¹/₂ white of leek
1 tablespoon margarine or oil

Soak the lentils overnight in the broth. The next day, peel and dice
the carrot, potato and onion and shred the washed leek. Sauté the
onion and leek in the margarine or oil until soft, then add the carrot
and potato and continue to cook for a further 5 minutes. Add the
lentils and broth, bring to a boil, then simmer for about 40 minutes or
until the lentils are soft. Purée if wished.

Trio of Vegetables with Ricotta

This is a tasty vegetable purée which can also be made with cream or cottage cheese. Combine avocado with ricotta and fresh herbs for another quick and easy recipe.

MAKES 6 PORTIONS

½ cup each broccoli and cauliflower flowerets, washed

1 zucchini, washed and sliced
3 tablespoons ricotta cheese

Steam the vegetables until tender, 8–10 minutes. Make into a purée together with the ricotta.

Creamed Cauliflower with Peanut Butter

Peanut butter is a good source of protein and is very popular with babies and toddlers.

MAKES 8 PORTIONS

2½ tablespoons basmati rice
1¼ cups cauliflower flowerets, washed

½ cup milk
1 tablespoon peanut butter

Cook the rice for about 15 minutes until soft. Meanwhile cook the cauliflower in milk for about 10 minutes. Blend the cauliflower, milk, rice and peanut butter to a smooth purée.

Special Spinach and Potato Purée

This purée makes a tasty introduction to spinach for your baby. It also makes a nice vegetable side dish for adults.

MAKES 14 PORTIONS

1 onion, peeled and finely chopped
2 tablespoons margarine
4 cups spinach, washed, chopped and tough stalks removed

1 large or 2 small potatoes, peeled and diced
¹/₂ cup chicken broth (see page 62)

Sauté the onion in the margarine over a low heat for 4–5 minutes until soft. Add the spinach and potato, pour in the broth and simmer slowly for about 35 minutes. Purée in a blender.

Oat and Vegetable Purée

Oats add bulk to the vegetable purée making it a satisfying meal.

MAKES 20 PORTIONS

1 celery stalk
1 white part of leek, washed carefully
2 medium or 4 small carrots

¹/₂ cup each of diced rutabaga, cauliflower and broccoli flowerets
3 tablespoons oatmeal
1 tablespoon chopped parsley

Peel, trim as appropriate and finely chop all the vegetables. Just cover the vegetables with water in a saucepan and add the oatmeal. Bring the water to a boil, then cover and simmer for about 20 minutes or until the vegetables are tender. Purée in a blender until the desired consistency. Mix in the chopped parsley.

Trio of Cauliflower, Red Bell Pepper and Corn

If you want to freeze a dish containing corn, you should use either fresh or canned corn in your recipe – frozen corn should not be re-frozen. Always purée corn in a mill for young babies to get rid of the tough outer skin.

MAKES 10 PORTIONS

1 cup cauliflower flowerets
½ cup milk

¼ cup chopped red bell pepper
½ cup corn kernels

Put the cauliflower in a saucepan with the milk and cook over a low heat for about 12 minutes until tender. Meanwhile, cook the red pepper and corn in water in a saucepan for about 6 minutes until tender. Drain the corn and pepper. Purée together with the cauliflower and milk in a food mill.

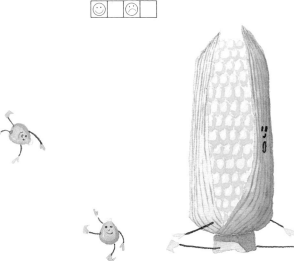

Cauliflower Cheese

This is a great favorite with babies. Try using different cheeses or combinations of cheese until you find your baby's favorite taste. Try using the cheese sauce over a mixture of vegetables as well.

MAKES 15 PORTIONS

1½ cups cauliflower flowerets

Cheese sauce
1 tablespoon margarine
1 tablespoon cornstarch
¾ cup milk
½ cup grated Cheddar, Edam or
Swiss cheese

Wash the cauliflower flowerets carefully and steam until tender (about 10 minutes). Meanwhile, for the sauce, melt the margarine over a gentle heat in a heavy-bottomed saucepan and stir in the cornstarch to make a smooth paste. Add the milk and stir until thickened. Take the saucepan off the heat and stir in the grated cheese. Keep stirring until all the cheese has melted and the sauce is smooth.

Add the cauliflower to the sauce and purée in a blender for younger babies. For older babies, mash with a fork or chop into little pieces.

Zucchini Gratin

This creamy purée is also good using green beans or broccoli.

MAKES 18 PORTIONS

1 medium potato, about 4 oz, peeled
1 medium zucchini, sliced
¹/₂ cup milk

¹/₄ cup grated Swiss cheese
1 sprig of parsley, chopped
a little margarine

Boil the potato until soft then drain. Steam the zucchini for 8 minutes. Purée all together in a food mill or blender.

Leek and Potato Purée with Ricotta

This is Lara's favorite vegetable purée. It also makes a superb vegetable soup for adults.

MAKES 16 PORTIONS

2 tablespoons margarine or oil
1¹/₂ cups leeks, carefully washed and sliced

2 cups potatoes, peeled and diced
2 cups chicken broth (see page 62)
2 tablespoons ricotta

Heat the margarine in a heavy-based pan. Add the leeks and cook over a gentle heat for 10 minutes until softened, stirring occasionally. Add the diced potatoes and broth and simmer, covered, for 25–30 minutes until tender. Purée and stir in the ricotta.

Tasty Lettuce and Zucchini Purée

When I experimented with this combination, the baby purée that I made turned out to be so good that I increased the quantities and made a delicious soup for the whole family. It is very healthful and low in calories too!

MAKES 4 PORTIONS

½ onion, peeled and finely chopped
1 tablespoon margarine or oil
½ cup zucchini, washed, trimmed and thinly sliced

2 cups shredded iceberg lettuce
¼ cup chicken broth (see page 62)

Sauté the onion in the margarine over a low heat for about 3 minutes until soft. Add the zucchini and lettuce and continue to cook over a low heat for 3 minutes. Pour over the chicken broth and cook, covered, for a further 3 minutes.

Purée in a blender until the desired consistency for your baby. As a soup for the whole family, I think it is better if it is not too smooth.

Minestrone

This is a very versatile recipe, as you can add rice, pasta or almost any vegetable. I find the flavor is best if you use chicken broth. For older children and adults, I like to add 2 teaspoons of tomato paste.

MAKES 7 ADULT PORTIONS OR 40 BABY PORTIONS

1 tablespoon margarine or oil
1/2 small onion, peeled and chopped
1 carrot, peeled and chopped
1/2 celery stalk, chopped
1/2 white of leek, chopped
1 cup shredded cabbage
5 cups water, chicken or vegetable broth (see pages 62 and 33)

1 cup peeled and diced potato
3 tablespoons shelled peas
1 tablespoon chopped parsley
1/3 cup small pasta shapes (optional)

Heat the margarine in a saucepan and fry the onion for 1 minute, then add the carrot, celery and leek. Sauté these for 2 minutes, then add the cabbage and continue to cook for another 4 minutes.

Cover with the water or broth. Add the potato, peas and chopped parsley and cook over a gentle heat for 20–25 minutes until the vegetables are soft and easy for your baby to chew (for younger babies, you can mash or purée the vegetables). If you want pasta in the soup, then add this 10 minutes prior to the end of cooking.

FISH

Fish with Fennel

The aniseed taste of fennel blends well with fish – see how your baby likes this new taste.

MAKES 7 PORTIONS

⅝ cup chopped Florence fennel
¾ cup chopped potato
½ cup chicken broth
4 oz white fish, skinned

1 tablespoon minced onion
½ bay leaf
a little margarine
milk

Put the fennel and potato in a saucepan and add the broth. Simmer for 15–20 minutes until the vegetables are soft. Meanwhile put the fish in an ovenproof dish, add the onion, bay leaf, dot with margarine and pour over enough milk to cover. Cook in an oven preheated to 350°F for 20 minutes. (Alternately cook in the microwave on High for about 3 minutes.) Flake the fish, making sure there are no bones and blend it with the vegetables and enough broth to make a smooth purée.

☺ ☹

Flounder in Cheese Sauce

Fish and cheese sauce go really well together, and the combination is always popular. Add some chives and you give an old recipe a new taste.

MAKES 8 PORTIONS

1 flounder, filleted and skinned
¹/₂ cup milk
1 sprig of parsley
1 celery stalk, chopped
1 tablespoon chopped onion

Cheese sauce
2 tablespoons margarine
¹/₄ cup all-purpose flour
¹/₂ cup milk
³/₄ cup grated Cheddar cheese
1 teaspoon snipped chives or chopped parsley

Put the flounder fillets in an ovenproof dish, pour the milk over and surround the fish with the parsley, celery and onion. Cover with aluminum foil and cook in an oven preheated to 350°F for about 20 minutes, or until the fish just flakes with a fork. Strain and reserve the milk and discard the vegetables.

To prepare the sauce, melt the margarine in a small saucepan and stir in the flour. Cook for 1 minute then stir in the milk and reserved cooking milk gradually until you have a smooth white sauce. Take the saucepan off the heat and stir in the cheese. When all the cheese has melted, add the snipped chives or parsley.

Flake the fish with a fork and make sure there are no stray bones. Add the fish to the cheese sauce and put it through the food mill to make it into a smooth purée for your baby.

Flounder with Spinach and Cheese

This makes a very tasty dark green fish purée. You could use Swiss cheese instead.

MAKES 8 PORTIONS

1 flounder, filleted and skinned
1 tablespoon milk
1 bay leaf
a little margarine

1 cup shredded spinach, washed and
tough stalks removed
1 cup grated Cheddar cheese

Put the flounder fillets with the milk and bay leaf in an ovenproof dish. Dot with margarine and cover with foil. Cook in an oven preheated to 350°F for 20 minutes. Alternately, cover with a lid and microwave for about 3 minutes on High.

Meanwhile cook the spinach in boiling water (about 10 minutes), then drain well and squeeze out any excess water. Discard the bay leaf and put all the remaining ingredients in a food processor, blend for about 1 minute and serve as a purée.

Fillet of Cod with Zucchini

Cooking fish and vegetables wrapped in foil in the oven is a good way of sealing in the natural flavor. Cutlets of fish (on the bone) are also very good cooked this way. Experiment using a variety of different vegetables. For older children, replace the milk with lemon or orange juice.

MAKES 3 PORTIONS

1 medium zucchini, washed and
trimmed
75 g/3 oz fillet of cod, skinned

1 sprig of fresh thyme
2 tablespoons milk
2 teaspoons olive oil

Cut the zucchini into small strips. Lay the fish on a piece of aluminum foil together with the zucchini and thyme, sprinkle with milk and olive oil and fold up into a parcel. Cook in an oven preheated to 350°F for about 20 minutes. Before serving, flake the fish with a fork. Make sure there are no bones and remove the thyme. Purée the vegetables and fish with the cooking liquid to the desired consistency.

☺ ☹

Creamy Fish with Cheese and Cornflakes

The white sauce on page 68 is used for this recipe and makes a good base for many different sauces.

MAKES 7 PORTIONS

4 oz fillet of white fish, skinned
milk
³/₄ cup Creamy Pasta Sauce (see page 68)

¹/₄ cup grated Cheddar cheese
¹/₂ cup crushed cornflakes

Put the fish in an ovenproof dish with just enough milk to cover. Bake at 350°F for 20 minutes or cook in the microwave on High for about 3 minutes. Drain off the cooking liquid. Pour the pasta sauce over the fish and sprinkle with the cheese and cornflakes. Return to the oven for about 8 minutes. Purée in a blender.

CHICKEN

Chicken Broth and My First Chicken Purée

Recipes taste much better if you use home-made chicken broth rather than a bouillon cube. I make it in large batches, divide it up into small containers, and keep it in the freezer to use as a base for soups, and chicken and vegetable purées.

MAKES APPROXIMATELY 5 PINTS

1 boiling fowl, plus giblets
2 parsnips
1 small turnip
3 carrots

2 leeks
2 large onions
1 celery stalk
3 sprigs of parsley

Cut the chicken into eight pieces, trimming excess fat. Trim, peel and wash the vegetables as necessary. Put the chicken pieces into a large saucepan together with the giblets. Cover generously with water, bring to a boil and skim the froth from the top. Add the vegetables and parsley and simmer for about 3½ hours. It is best to remove the chicken breasts after about 1½ hours if you are going to eat them, otherwise they will become too dry.)

Leave in the fridge overnight and remove any congealed fat from the top in the morning. Strain out all the chicken and vegetables to make the chicken broth. Season to taste.

You can purée some of the chicken breast in a mill together with a selection of the vegetables and some broth to make a chicken and vegetable purée for your baby, or purée the vegetables and broth for a non-clear soup for adults!

☺ ☹

Chicken with Cottage Cheese

Babies of this age are a little too young to eat pieces of chicken as finger food. This and the following four recipes show you simple ways of transforming cold chicken into tasty food for your baby.

MAKES 6 PORTIONS

½ cup cooked boneless chicken, chopped
1 tablespoon plain yogurt

1½ tablespoons cottage cheese with pineappple

Mix together the chicken, yogurt and cottage cheese. Put through a mill to make a smooth purée.

Chicken with Rice and Beans

MAKES 10 PORTIONS

¾ cup green beans
½ cup brown rice
3 tablespoons apple juice

½ cup cooked boneless chicken, chopped

Steam the beans until tender and cook the rice in water (about 20 minutes). Mix all the ingredients together and blend in a food processor. Put through a food mill to make a smooth purée. (You can add more apple juice if it is too thick.)

White Chicken Purée

MAKES 6 PORTIONS

1 medium potato, peeled
²/₃ cup cauliflower flowerets
2 tablespoons milk

½ cup cooked boneless chicken,
chopped

Boil the potato until soft. Steam the cauliflower above the potato for the last 10 minutes. Mash the potato and cauliflower with the milk, then add the chicken. Make into a purée in the blender. (If too thick, add a little extra milk.)

Chicken Salad Purée

What could be simpler. For toddlers, chop the ingredients and mix with mayonnaise or salad cream.

MAKES 4 PORTIONS

¼ cup cooked boneless chicken,
chopped
1 chunk of cucumber
4 seedless grapes, skinned
2 tablespoons plain yogurt or cottage
cheese
1 teaspoon chopped chives
1 slice avocado

Put all the ingredients into a blender and purée until the desired consistency.

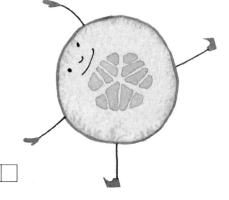

Chicken and Peach Delight

This is a delicious combination; it's very simple to make and popular with young children of all ages.

MAKES 10 PORTIONS

¹/₂ cup cooked boneless chicken, chopped
¹/₄ cup cooked brown rice
1 ripe peach

1 tablespoon peach juice
1 tablespoon milk
2 teaspoons wheatgerm

Just mix all the ingredients together and chop roughly in the food processor.

☺ ☹

Chicken and Mixed Vegetable Purée

This purée makes a very tasty introduction to chicken for your baby. Made in larger quantities, and seasoned after the baby's portions have been removed to be puréed, this makes a super family meal.

MAKES 15 PORTIONS

1 single chicken breast or 2 thighs, skinned and off the bone
¹/₂ celery stalk, chopped
1 carrot, peeled and diced

1-inch white of leek, shredded
1 potato, peeled and diced
a sprig of parsley
1 cup chicken broth

Cut the chicken into pieces and put it into a small flameproof casserole dish or saucepan together with the vegetables, parsley and chicken broth. Simmer gently for 30 minutes, then purée to the desired consistency.

☺ ☹

Chicken with Grapes and Zucchini

The addition of grapes to this recipe gives the chicken a little
sweetness which babies love. It is very simple to make and is
usually gobbled up pretty quickly.

MAKES 8 PORTIONS

*1 single chicken breast or 2 thighs,
skinned and off the bone
a good ¹/₂ cup home-made chicken
broth (see page 62)*

*8 green grapes, skinned and seeds
removed
1 zucchini, washed and sliced
1 tablespoon baby rice*

Cut the chicken into pieces. Put all the ingredients except the baby
rice into a small saucepan and simmer for 30 minutes. Purée to
the desired consistency and thicken by stirring in the baby rice.

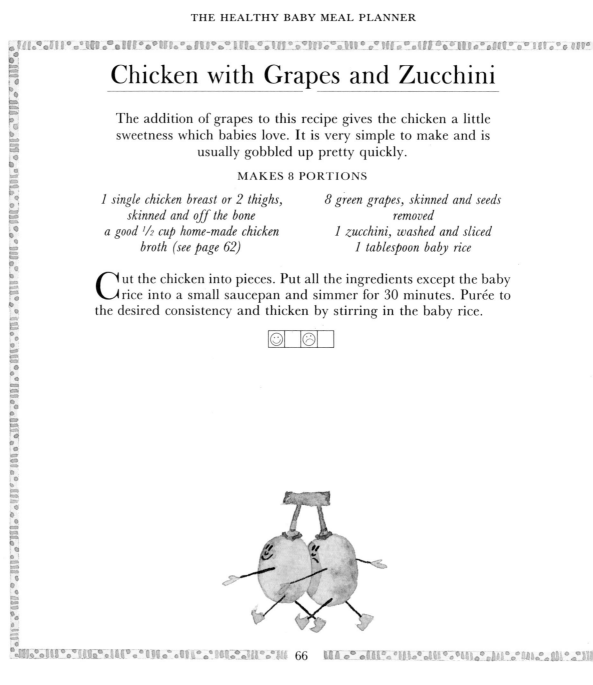

Mango Chicken

Mango gives a lovely sweet taste to the chicken which babies love.

MAKES 6 PORTIONS

*1 single chicken breast or 2 thighs,
on the bone, trimmed
margarine or oil, for frying*

*½ onion, thinly sliced
½ ripe mango, peeled and sliced
¾ cup chicken broth*

Sauté the chicken in margarine for about 8 minutes until golden. Add the onion slices halfway through. Put the chicken, onion and mango in a saucepan with the broth. Simmer for 30 minutes until chicken is cooked. Take the chicken off the bone and chop or purée with the sauce.

Chicken Liver Special

Liver is one of the best foods you can give your baby. Find a liver recipe that your baby enjoys, and make it again and again.

MAKES 6 PORTIONS

*2 chicken livers, cleaned and trimmed
2 teaspoons chopped carrot
2 teaspoons chopped white of leek
1 tablespoon chopped rutabaga*

*½ cup chicken broth (see
page 62)
1 potato, peeled*

Cook the chicken livers together with the chopped vegetables in the broth for about 8 minutes over a low heat. Meanwhile, boil the potato until tender. Mash the potato. Purée the liver and vegetables together with the potato. The chicken broth makes this into quite a creamy purée.

PASTA

Creamy Pasta Sauce

Use this sauce plain, with grated cheese, or vegetable purée.

MAKES 4 PORTIONS OF SAUCE

1-inch celery, chopped
1-inch carrot, chopped
a small piece of onion
½ bay leaf

a few peppercorns
¾ cup milk
1 tablespoon butter or margarine
1 tablespoon all-purpose flour

Add the vegetables, bay leaf and peppercorns to the milk in a saucepan and bring to a boil. Remove from the heat and allow to infuse for 30 minutes. Strain the milk. Melt the butter, mix in the flour to make a paste and gradually stir in the flavored milk. Bring to a boil over a low heat, stirring, to make a thick white sauce.

Sweet Green Pea Sauce

MAKES 2 PORTIONS OF SAUCE

⅓ cup fresh or frozen peas
½ tablespoon minced onion

½ tablespoon margarine

Cook the peas in ½ cup water for 5 minutes or until tender. Sauté the onion in margarine until soft. Drain the peas, reserving 2 tablespoons liquid. Purée the peas, liquid and onion in a mill.

Creamy Chicken Sauce

First make the recipe for Creamy Pasta Sauce on page 68, then make this simple chicken purée and combine the two for a special meal.

MAKES 8 PORTIONS OF SAUCE

1 single chicken breast on the bone
1¹/₂ cups water or chicken broth
¹/₄ cup chopped celery
¹/₄ cup chopped carrot

¹/₂ tablespoon chopped onion
a sprig of parsley
1 x Creamy Pasta Sauce (see page 68)

Put the chicken breast in a saucepan with the water or broth. Add the vegetables and parsley and simmer for 25 minutes or until the chicken is cooked. Take the chicken off the bone and purée with the vegetables and as much broth as necessary. Combine the chicken purée with the Creamy Pasta Sauce.

Green Pasta Sauce

MAKES 5 PORTIONS OF SAUCE

2 medium zucchini
¹/₂ cup sliced green beans

2 tablespoons chicken broth (see page 62)

Wash and slice the zucchini. Steam them with the beans for 8–10 minutes. Purée together with the chicken broth. Pour over cooked pasta and serve.

Creamy Eggplant Sauce

Before cooking, it is best to slice the eggplants and sprinkle them with salt to draw out the bitter flavors. Leave for 20 minutes and remember to wash the salt off well.

MAKES 6 PORTIONS

1 small eggplant (about 8 oz), peeled and sliced
1 tablespoon olive oil

¼ cup ricotta cheese
1 tablespoon milk

Fry the eggplant slices in hot olive oil until browned. When cooked wrap in paper towels to absorb excess oil. Purée the eggplant, ricotta and milk in a blender to to the required consistency.

Popeye Pasta

MAKES 8 PORTIONS

2 cups chopped spinach
½ cup shell-shaped pasta

⅓ cup grated Swiss cheese
2 tablespoons milk

Boil the spinach in a little water for about 5 minutes until tender. Meanwhile cook the pasta according to the instructions on the packet. Once the spinach is cooked press out all the excess water. Combine with the cheese, pasta and milk and blend to make into a purée or chop for older babies.

SIX TO NINE MONTH MEAL PLANNER

	Breakfast	Sleep	Lunch	Sleep	Dinner	Bedtime
Day 1	Chex with milk Mashed banana	Milk	My First Chicken Purée Grated apple Juice	Milk	Leek and Potato Purée Pear Water or juice	Milk
Day 2	Instant Oatmeal with milk Fruit purée Milk	Milk	Fish with Fennel Banana Juice	Milk	Pasta with Green Pasta Sauce Yogurt Water or juice	Milk
Day 3	Apple and Baby Cereal Toast Milk	Milk	Cauliflower Cheese Grated pear Juice	Milk	Spinach and Potato Purée Rusk Water or juice	Milk
Day 4	Baby cereal with milk Dried Apricot Purée Cottage Cheese	Milk	Lentil Purée Peaches and Rice Juice	Milk	Minestrone Toast Water or juice	Milk
Day 5	Chex with milk Peaches, Apples and Pears	Milk	Pasta and Creamy Sauce Baked Banana Milk	Milk	My First Chicken Purée Pear Water or juice	Milk
Day 6	Baby cereal with milk Cottage Cheese and Sharon Fruit	Milk	Zucchini Gratin Home-made Fruit Gelatin Milk	Milk	Chicken with Rice and Beans Apple Water	Milk
Day 7	Oatmeal with milk Cottage Cheese and Sharon Fruit	Milk	Chicken Liver Special Apple, Prune and Sauce Juice	Milk	Tasty Lettuce and Zucchini Purée Papaya Water or juice	Milk

CHAPTER FOUR

NINE TO TWELVE MONTHS

Towards the end of the first year, babies' weight gain usually slows down quite dramatically. Quite often, babies who have been good eaters in the past become much more difficult to feed. Many refuse to be spoon-fed and want to assert their new-found independence, using their hands to feed themselves. My daughter at the age of ten months went through a phase of refusing to eat anything offered to her on a spoon. I was determined that she should eat the home-made purées I had prepared, so I gave her various finger foods like steamed carrots or strips of toast which I dipped into the purées. That way I succeeded in getting her to eat and enjoy them and everyone was happy.

Mealtime Patience

Let your baby experiment by allowing him or her to use a spoon. Most of the food will probably end up on you or on the floor, but with practise your baby's aim will get better! Put a waterproof tablecloth under the high chair to catch the food that falls on the floor. It is probably best to have two bowls of food and two spoons, one which you use to spoon-feed your baby, the other (preferably a bowl which sticks to the table by suction) for your baby to play with. You will need lots of patience at meal times, as many babies are very easily distracted at this stage and prefer to play with their food rather than eat it. If all else fails I find that if you can attract their attention by giving them a small toy to hold, you can sometimes slip food into their mouths on a spoon and they will eat without really noticing what they are doing and forget to put up any resistance!

No child under the age of one needs to drink cow's milk. For drinks continue using formula or breast milk, which has a much lower salt content and is complete with essential vitamins. However, as solid food intake increases, milk need no longer form such a staple part of your child's diet, although she should still be drinking a minimum of 20 fl oz (2½ cups) of milk a day (or the equivalent as dairy products or in cooking). It is an important source of protein and calcium. Many mothers assume that when their baby cries it is because she wants more milk but often babies of this age are given *too much* milk and not enough solid food. If you fill your baby's stomach with milk when she really wants some solid food, you will not get a very satisfied baby.

If you have a juice extractor, you can make all sorts of wonderful fruit and vegetable drinks for your baby – try combinations like apple and banana juice. Your baby should now be drinking happily from a cup, the bottle kept for her bedtime drink of warm milk.

Your baby will be teething at this age and very often sore gums can put her off eating for a while. Don't worry, she will make up for this later that day or the next day. (Rubbing a teething gel on your baby's gums, or giving her something very cold to chew, can help relieve soreness and restore appetite.)

It is a good idea to eat something with your baby at meal times. There are some mothers who sit opposite their babies and try to spoon food into their mouths while eating nothing themselves. Babies are great mimics and more likely to enjoy eating if they see you tucking in as well.

The Foods to Choose

You can be a little more adventurous with the food that you make for your baby. It is a good idea now to develop her tastes for garlic and herbs, both of which are very healthful. Children tend to be less fussy eaters if they are introduced to a wide range of foods early. Again, if your baby dislikes certain foods, never force her to eat them; just leave out those foods and perhaps re-introduce them in a couple of months' time. Try also to vary the foods as much as possible, as this will lead to a more balanced diet. If you give your child a favorite food too often, it is possible she will go off it altogether.

Your baby can soon eat berry fruits (but these should still be put through a mill in the earlier stages to get rid of the indigestible seeds). Fruit gelatins will be interesting for your baby to look at, feel and eat. Your baby will like fruit and vegetables that have been grated.

Oily fish can now be introduced; it contains iron and fat-soluble vitamins which white fish does not. All fish must obviously be very fresh. Chicken dishes can become more interesting in both texture and tastes and the types of pasta cooked can be large enough for the independent baby to pick up (butterflies, spirals, shells and animal shapes are good). Increase the quantity per serving of pasta to about $\frac{1}{2}$–$\frac{3}{4}$ cup cooked ($\frac{1}{4}$–$\frac{3}{8}$ cup dry).

Whenever possible, try to make the food look attractive on the plate. Choose contrasting colors and arrange the food in pretty shapes. You can use your imagination to make little faces or animals. Never pile too much food on to the plate but give a second helping – your baby will let you know in no uncertain terms if she wants more.

MEAT

A good red meat to introduce is liver, which is one of the most nutritious foods you can give your baby. It is the richest natural source of iron and is easily digested. If you do not like liver, try not to show it. Your reaction can easily put her off eating it. Be careful not to overcook liver or it will become tough and impossible for the baby to chew. Both my children enjoy eating liver, which surprised my husband and I (neither of us can bear the taste)!

Beef is the best red meat, I think, as it is less fatty than lamb. Although lamb and pork are both suitable around 1 year. Always choose lean cuts and make sure it is thoroughly cooked. After cooking ground meat for young babies, I find that if I chop it in a food processor for 30 seconds, it becomes much softer and easier to chew.

Textures and Quantities

It is easy to get into the habit of only giving your baby soft foods but you should try to vary the consistency of food that you give your baby. There is no need to purée all foods. Babies do not need teeth to be able to chew; gums do a great job on foods that are not too hard. Give some food mashed (fish), some grated (cheese), some diced (carrots) and some whole (pieces of chicken, slices of toast and pieces of raw fruit).

As far as quantities are concerned, you must let your baby's appetite be your guide. The portions in the recipes are a guide to what an average baby of this age would eat (two to three ice-cube-sized blocks, no longer singles).

You could start to freeze food in larger containers, like empty yogurt pots, well covered with foil or plastic bags.

Finger Foods

By the age of nine months, your baby will probably want to start feeding herself. It is a good idea therefore to start giving her some foods that are easy for her to eat with her fingers. Finger foods are great for keeping your child occupied while you prepare her proper meal – or you could make a whole meal of finger foods.

Never leave your child unattended while eating. It is very easy for a baby to choke on even very small pieces of food. Avoid giving your baby whole nuts, fruits with pits, whole grapes, ice cubes, olives and any other foods that might get stuck in her throat.

RAW FRUIT
Always peel fruit and make sure any pits or seeds have been removed. If your baby finds it difficult to chew, give soft fruits

that melt in the mouth like bananas or peaches or grated fruits.

Berry and citrus fruits should only be introduced in very quantities as your baby nears one year. Remove as much of the pith as possible.

Many babies who are teething really enjoy biting into fruit. A banana put into the freezer for a few hours makes an excellent teething aid for young babies. Once your baby is able to hold food successfully give her larger pieces of fruit and encourage her to bite little bits off. (But don't let her *store* these in her mouth; on occasion I had to resort to opening my son's mouth and removing food which he refused to swallow!) If your baby has only a few teeth, then it is a good idea to give her grated fruit.

FRUITY IDEAS
apples, apricots, avocado pear, banana, cherries, blueberries, grapes, kiwi fruit, mango, melon, nectarine, papaya, peach, pear, plum.
Later on raspberries, strawberries, orange, tomato

DRIED FRUITS
Dried fruits are an excellent source of iron. If the fruit is too hard for your baby to chew, soften it first by soaking it in boiling water.

Do not give a lot of dried fruit as it can be difficult to digest, and laxative in effect. This is particularly true of raisins including golden raisins (although babies love them!).

MORE FRUITY IDEAS
apple rings, banana chips, apricots, dates, peaches, pears, prunes, raisins, golden raisins, yogurt- or carob-coated raisins
---

VEGETABLES

To begin with, give your baby soft cooked vegetables cut into pieces that are easy for her to hold, and encourage her to bite off little pieces. (It is best to steam vegetables as this will help to preserve Vitamin C.) Gradually cook the vegetables for less time so that your baby gets used to having to chew harder. Once your baby has good coordination, she will enjoy picking up little vegetables like peas and corn.

Once your baby has mastered the art of feeding herself cooked vegetables, you can introduce carefully washed grated raw vegetables and sticks of raw vegetables. Even if your baby is unable to bite into these sticks, she will enjoy chewing on them as an aid to teething. In fact sticks of raw vegetables such as carrots and cucumber are very soothing for sore gums if they are chilled in the freezer or in iced water for a few minutes. Large pieces of raw vegetables are safer than small pieces as a baby will nibble off what she can manage, whereas a small piece put into her mouth whole could cause her to choke if she tried to swallow it.

Try giving your baby cooked corn cobs once he or she can chew well. Cut the corn in half or into three pieces or look out for little mini-sized corn cobs in some supermarkets – just right for babies. Corn is fun to eat and babies love to hold and chew it.

Vegetables are also very good dipped into sauces and purées. Try using some of the recipes for vegetable purées as dipping sauces.

VEGETABLE VARIETY
eggplant, beans (green), broccoli, Brussels sprouts, cabbage, carrots, cauliflower, celery, corn cobs (and kernels and baby corn), zucchini, snowpeas, mushrooms, peas, potato, rutabaga, bell pepper, sweet potato
---

BREADS AND RUSKS

Pieces of toast, rusks and firm bread can be dipped into purées and sauces. Often a baby who refuses to be spoon-fed will eat her meal by sucking it off a rusk or a piece of toast.

Many baby rusks on the market contain as much sugar as a cookie and even so-called low-sugar rusks can contain more than 15 per cent sugar. It is very easy to make your own sugar-free alternate from wholewheat bread.

For savory home-made rusks, simply cut a thick (½-inch) slice of wholewheat (cracked wheat or rye) bread into three strips. Melt ⅛ teaspoon Vegemite in 1 teaspoon boiling water, or use strong bouillon and brush this evenly over the bread strips. Bake in the oven preheated to 350°F for 15 minutes. You can leave out the Vegemite if your baby prefers and you can prepare a store of rusks in advance and keep them in an airtight container for 3 or 4 days.

Rice cakes come in all different flavors and are excellent for teething, as they seem to hold together well.

MINIATURE SANDWICHES
Little sandwiches cut into fingers, squares, small triangles or even animal shapes with a cookie cutter are very popular with babies. There are some suggestions for fillings below and see the toddler section for a more exhaustive list (pages 186–187).

FILLING SUGGESTIONS
mashed banana
peanut butter and apple purée
chopped chicken with fruit chutney
cottage cheese and grated apple
cream cheese and strawberry jelly
Vegemite and grated cheese
grated cheese and grated cucumber
mashed sardines with lettuce

BREAKFAST CEREALS
Babies love to pick up and eat little pieces of breakfast cereal. Try to choose cereals that are fortified with iron and vitamins and which do not have added sugar.

GOOD MORNING MUNCHIES
Cheerios, Cornflakes, Granola, Chex, Grahams

CHEESE
Start by giving your baby grated cheese or cut wafer-thin slices. Once she has mastered chewing, you can move on to chunks and strips of cheese. I have found that the following cheeses are especially popular: Cheddar, mozzarella, Edam, Swiss and Monterey Jack. Cream cheese, ricotta and cottage cheeses are also very popular. Keep away from strong cheeses like blue cheese, Brie and Camembert. Always make sure that the cheese you give your baby is pasteurised.

PASTA
Pasta comes in all shapes and sizes, it is soft to chew and is very appealing to babies. I have given some recipes for pasta sauces but most of the vegetable purées can also be served with pasta. You can try sprinkling a little grated cheese over the pasta as well.

My children enjoy eating spaghetti as finger food!

MEAT

Slices or chunks of cooked chicken (or turkey) make great finger food. As well as plain pieces of chicken, try giving your baby chicken cooked in a sauce. Very often the sauce makes the chicken more tender and so it is easier for your baby to chew.

Miniature chicken balls are another favorite (try my recipe for Chicken and Apple Balls, page 98). Your baby may also enjoy chewing on miniature drumsticks. Remove the skin and make sure that your baby avoids eating any pieces of bone. There is a fine needle-like bone in all drumsticks which is potentially very dangerous – extra care needs to be taken with drumsticks.

Strips of sautéed liver make good finger food as they are easy to hold and soft to eat. Try, too, some miniature meatballs (see page 154). Pieces of steak and chunks of meat are generally too tough for young babies to chew.

FISH

Pieces of flaked white fish are good as they are low in fat, high in protein and easy for your child to chew. You can give them to your baby either plain or mixed with a sauce. Do take extra care when serving fish to your baby in any recipe to check the fish thoroughly for bones before you cook it and when flaking it.

Make your own fish fingers and fish balls (see pages 94, 133–134).

Breakfast

The first meal of the day is important to all of us after a night's fasting, particularly so to energetic babies and toddlers!

Recipes can now contain more interesting and more nutritious grains. Wheatgerm is particularly good and can be sprinkled on to cereals or yogurt. Mixing cereals and fruit makes a delicious and nutritious start to the day. Many of the home-made cereals can be mixed with apple juice instead of milk.

Recent research has shown that oat bran (available in health-food stores) can prevent the build up of cholesterol in the blood (even in young children) and you can easily include this in your baking for the whole family.

Highly refined, sugar-coated cereals should be avoided. Do not be fooled by the list of added vitamins on the side of the box – unprocessed cereals are much healthier for your child.

Individual packets of cereals are great fun for your baby. She can nibble from the box and once it is empty it is fun to play with too. Choosing different cereals to combine can brighten the morning.

There are also some recipes in the toddler baking and fruit dessert sections which make excellent breakfast food: Bran Muffins with Apples and Raisins (page 175); Funny Shape Biscuits (page 178), Snow-Covered Fruit Salad (page 165), or Banana Split (page 164).

BREAKFAST

Fruity Swiss Muesli

You can vary the fruit in this muesli, adding, for example, sliced peaches or bananas instead of grapes. It can be served with or without milk. Make this for the whole family.

MAKES 6 ADULT PORTIONS

1 cup wheatgerm
1 cup oatmeal
2 cups unsweetened apple juice
2 teaspoons lemon juice (optional)

1 tablespoon brown sugar
2 apples, peeled, cored and chopped
2 pears, peeled, cored and chopped
3 cups grapes, halved and seeded

Combine the wheatgerm, oatmeal and apple juice, cover and refrigerate overnight. Next morning, stir in the lemon juice, brown sugar, chopped apples and pears, place in a food processor and switch on for 30 seconds. Put the muesli into a serving bowl and add the grapes.

Fruity Yogurt

Many commercial fruit yogurts have a lot of added sugar. It is easy to make your own, adding a combination of your baby's favorite foods.

MAKES 2 ADULT PORTIONS

2 tablespoons mixed ripe chopped fruit
1/2 teaspoon vanilla extract

1/2 cup plain yogurt
2 tablespoons apple juice
1 teaspoon wheatgerm

Mix everything together except for the wheatgerm which you sprinkle on top. (Purée the fruit first for younger babies.)

Easy Fruit Brunch

This takes a minute to prepare and is quite delicious.

MAKES 4 ADULT PORTIONS

2 bananas, peeled
1 cup plain yogurt
2 tablespoons cream cheese
2 tablespoons heavy cream

1/4 cup canned prunes, pitted
a pinch powdered cinnamon

Simply mix all the ingredients together except for the cinnamon and a few reserved banana slices and blend until smooth. Decorate with slices of banana and the cinnamon.

Fruit Compote

I like to serve this cold with yogurt for breakfast but it could also
be served hot with ice-cream for dessert.

MAKES 4 ADULT PORTIONS

$^3/_4$ cup each of pitted prunes and dried
apricots
1 cup dried apples
$^1/_3$ cup each dried figs and golden
raisins
$^3/_4$ cup cranberry or apple juice

$^7/_8$ cup water
$^1/_4$ cinnamon stick
$1^1/_2$ fresh pears, peeled, cored and
diced
$^3/_8$ cup plain yogurt

Combine dried fruits, juice, water and spice in a heavy-bottomed
saucepan, bring to a boil, reduce heat and simmer, covered, for
30 minutes. Add the diced fresh pears and simmer for another 10
minutes. Discard the cinnamon stick and leave compote to cool.
Serve cold with the yogurt.

Cornflakes with Apples

MAKES 2 PORTIONS

2 tablespoons cornflakes
2 tablespoons apple purée (see
page 24)

2 tablespoons plain yogurt

Put all the ingredients into a food processor and blend until well
mixed (about 30 seconds).

Apple Muesli

You can vary the recipe by combining different fruits and, later on, your toddler may enjoy a few well-chopped nuts.

MAKES 4–5 ADULT PORTIONS

1¹/₃ cups oatmeal
2 tablespoons golden raisins
1¹/₂ cups natural apple or apple and pear juice

2 dessert apples, peeled, cored and grated
milk to mix

Mix the oatmeal, golden raisins and apple juice in a bowl, cover and leave to soak overnight in the fridge. In the morning, stir in the grated apple and enough milk to make the muesli soft and moist.

Mixed Cereal Muesli

As your child gets older you can let her help make up her very own muesli recipe using her favorite breakfast cereals and fruit.

MAKES 2 ADULT PORTIONS

1 tablespoon Cheerios
1 tablespoon Bran Flakes
1 tablespoon Graham crackers, crushed
4 slices of canned peaches, cut into chunks

¹/₂ tablespoon raisins
¹/₂ small apple, peeled, cored and cut into chunks
2 teaspoons wheatgerm

Mix all the ingredients together, altering the cereals and fruit to taste, and serve with milk.

Cornflakes with Yogurt

I find that children love their own individual portions of food, and my two like to eat dry cornflakes from the miniature packets. If I put cornflakes into a bowl and add milk, they won't touch them! This and Cornflakes with Apples (page 81) are good for older babies who are lazy at chewing and prefer their food puréed.

MAKES 2 PORTIONS

2 tablespoons cornflakes
½ cup plain or vanilla yogurt

2 teaspoons strawberry jelly, warmed

Put all the ingredients into a food processor and blend until well mixed (about 30 seconds).

Matzo Brei

For those of you who have never heard of *matzo*, it is a large square of unleavened bread similar to crispbread. When uncooked, it is very brittle and Nicholas loves to snap it into pieces and strew it all over the floor. This is why I prefer to give it to him cooked!

MAKES 2 ADULT PORTIONS

1 matzo
1 egg, beaten

2 tablespoons margarine
a pinch of sugar (optional)

Break the *matzo* into small pieces and soak for a couple of minutes in cold water. Squeeze out the excess water then add the *matzo* to the beaten egg. Melt the margarine in a frying pan until sizzling and fry the *matzo* on both sides. Sprinkle with sugar if wished.

French Toast

French toast can be served with a variety of toppings such as maple syrup, peanut butter or jelly. For a change, you could add cinnamon instead of vanilla, then blend a ripe banana with the milk and soak the bread in the banana mixture before frying.

MAKES 2 ADULT PORTIONS

1 egg
½ cup milk
¼ teaspoon vanilla extract

2 slices white, raisin or wheatmeal bread
a little margarine

Beat the egg lightly and add milk and vanilla. Soak the bread in the mixture. Melt the margarine in a frying pan and fry the slices of bread on both sides until golden brown. Wheatmeal bread slices are more fragile than white bread and can break very easily.

Cheese Scramble

You could use cottage cheese instead of Cheddar cheese.

MAKES 1 ADULT PORTION

1 egg
1 tablespoon milk
1 tablespoon margarine

1 tablespoon finely grated Cheddar cheese
1 tomato, skinned and seeded (optional)

Beat the egg with the milk. Melt the margarine over a low heat then add the egg mixture. Cook slowly, stirring all the time. When the mixture has thickened and looks soft and creamily set, add the cheese and chopped tomato. Serve immediately.

FRUIT

Baked Apples with Raisins

Tart apples have a better flavor but dessert apples are sweeter. You can use either for this recipe. The apples are delicious served with ice cream or custard sauce.

MAKES 6 PORTIONS

2 apples
½ cup apple juice or water
2 tablespoons raisins

a little powdered cinnamon
2 teaspoons maple sirup (if using tart apples)
a little butter or margarine

Core the apples and prick the skins with a fork to stop them bursting. Put the apples in an ovenproof dish and pour the apple juice or water around the base. Put 1 tablespoon of the raisins into the center of each apple, sprinkle with cinnamon and pour over maple sirup (if using tart apples). Top each with a little butter. Bake in an oven preheated to 350°F for about 45 minutes.

For young babies scoop out the pulp of the apple and purée roughly with the raisins and some of the juices from the dish.

Apple and Blackberry

Blackberries and apples make a delicious combination, and the blackberries (which are rich in Vitamin C) turn the apples dark red. This also makes a super filling for a betty (see page 167).

MAKES 8 PORTIONS

2 tart apples, peeled, cored and sliced   *³/₄ cup blackberries*
superfine sugar to taste

Cook the apples with the blackberries in a saucepan with the sugar and 1 tablespoon water. Cook until the apples are soft (about 10 minutes). Put the fruit through a mill to make into a smooth purée.

Rice Pudding with Peaches

MAKES 8–10 PORTIONS

2¹/₂ cups milk   *1 cinnamon stick*
¹/₃ cup short-grain rice   *2 ripe peaches, skinned*
1 tablespoon each of vanilla and   *1 heaped tablespoon raisins*
brown sugars, or 2 tablespoons   *¹/₂ cup peach or apple juice*
superfine sugar

Bring the milk to a boil, add the rice, sugar and cinnamon stick and simmer, stirring occasionally, for about 1 hour, 40 minutes until tender. Alternately, bake in a buttered dish for about 2 hours at 300°F stirring after 30 minutes.

Meanwhile purée the peaches, and simmer the raisins in the peach or apple juice. When the rice pudding is cooked, stir in the peach purée, raisins and fruit juice.

Fresh Pear with Semolina

This recipe is also good with apricots or apple purée with cinnamon. If you do not have any semolina, you can add a finely crushed rusk to the milk (which does not need to be boiled).

MAKES 2 PORTIONS

1 tablespoon semolina
½ cup milk

1 ripe pear, peeled, cored and sliced

Put the semolina and milk in a saucepan, bring to a boil and simmer for 3–4 minutes. Add the pear, then put all the ingredients through a mill to make a purée or chop the pear finely.

Strawberry Rice Pudding

The secret of a good rice pudding is long, slow, gentle cooking. Make it after breakfast and it will be ready in time for lunch.

MAKES 6 PORTIONS

⅓ cup short-grain brown rice
¼ teaspoon vanilla extract
2 teaspoons strawberry jelly

2½ cups milk
a little butter

Put the rice, vanilla and strawberry jelly into a buttered ovenproof dish. Pour over the milk, dot with the butter, and cook in an oven heated to 300°F for 3 hours. Stir the mixture well after 30 minutes. Serve with extra strawberry jelly whirled into the rice pudding.

Cheese and Raisin Delight

This makes a delicious combination and is very nutritious.

MAKES 2 PORTIONS

½ small apple, peeled
¼ cup grated Swiss cheese

1½ tablespoons raisins
1 tablespoon plain yogurt

Grate the apple and mix in the Swiss cheese, raisins and yogurt. For young babies who do not chew, put all the ingredients in a blender for about 1 minute.

Yogurt with Dried Fruit

Serve this warm with some vanilla ice cream as a special treat.

MAKES 12 PORTIONS

1 cup dried apples
¾ cup natural apple juice
1 ripe pear, peeled, cored and chopped

½ cup canned prunes, pitted and drained
½ cup plain yogurt

Put the apples in a saucepan with the apple juice, bring to a boil and simmer for about 20 minutes. After 10 minutes add the pear pieces. Drain the apples and pear and put through a mill together with the prunes. Add the yogurt and mix it together with the fruit in a blender.

VEGETABLES

Oscar's Delight

So called because this recipe is the same green color as 'Oscar', the character from *Sesame Street*. If my son believes this is Oscar's favorite food he is much more likely to eat it himself. Calling food funny names is another way to encourage children to eat.

MAKES 10 PORTIONS

*1 medium zucchini, trimmed, washed
and sliced
1 cup cauliflower flowerets*

*³/₄ cup broccoli flowerets
¹/₄ cup grated Cheddar cheese
1 egg yolk*

Steam the vegetables for 7 minutes until tender, then purée with the cheese and egg yolk. Bake in a greased dish at 350°F for 15–20 minutes.

☺ ☹

Gratin of Carrots

You can also try this recipe with celery or fennel.

MAKES 6 PORTIONS

*³/₄ cup diced carrots
1 egg
¹/₂ cup milk*

*¹/₃ cup grated Swiss cheese
¹/₂ teaspoon fresh tarragon (optional)
a little margarine*

Make a carrot purée (see page 25), add remaining ingredients and bake as in recipe above for 10–15 minutes.

☺ ☹

Lentil and Vegetable Purée

This makes a delicious purée which my nine-month-old daughter loved. Lentils are an excellent source of protein and very easy to cook.

MAKES 10 PORTIONS

1 medium onion, finely chopped
²/₃ cup celery, trimmed and chopped
1 cup carrots, peeled and chopped

oil or margarine for frying
¹/₄ cup split red lentils
2¹/₂ cups vegetable broth (see page 33) or water

Fry the onion, celery and carrot in a little oil for about 10 minutes until tender. Add the lentils and pour over the broth or water. Simmer covered, for 20 minutes. Make into a purée in a blender or put through a mill.

☺ ☹

Multi-Colored Casserole

Babies love the bright colors and miniature size of these vegetables. It makes eating fun, and is a good lesson in finger control.

MAKES 6 PORTIONS

¹/₈ cup olive oil
4 shallots, peeled and finely chopped
1 red bell pepper, seeded and finely chopped

1 cup frozen peas
1¹/₂ cups frozen corn
1 cup grated Cheddar cheese
1 tablespoon finely chopped parsley

Heat the oil in a frying pan, add the shallots and red pepper and cook for 3 minutes. Meanwhile cook the peas and corn in boiling water for about 4 minutes, then drain. Put the vegetables into an ovenproof dish, sprinkle with the cheese and parsley and bake in the oven preheated to 350°F for 15 minutes.

Cabbage Surprise

This is a delicious recipe and very simple to prepare. It makes a great lunchtime meal for the whole family; just increase the quantities, sprinkle with extra grated cheese, either Cheddar or Parmesan and brown under the grill before serving. Alternately, mix all the cooked ingredients together and bake in the oven at 350°F for 15 minutes.

MAKES 6 PORTIONS

2¹/₂ tablespoons brown rice
1 cup shredded cabbage
1 small tomato, skinned, seeded and chopped

a little margarine or oil
¹/₂ cup grated Cheddar cheese

Cook the rice in water until quite soft (about 25 minutes). Boil the cabbage in water for about 5 minutes or until tender. Sauté the tomato in a little margarine, add the well drained cabbage and continue to cook for a further 2 minutes. Stir in the grated cheese and cook over a low heat until all the cheese has melted. Mix the cabbage, tomato and cheese together with the cooked rice and chop it into small pieces.

Vegetables in Cheese Sauce

MAKES 12 PORTIONS

1 cup cauliflower flowerets
1 carrot, peeled and thinly sliced
¹/₂ cup shelled peas
1 zucchini, washed and sliced

Cheese sauce
2 tablespoons margarine
1¹/₂ tablespoons all-purpose flour
¹/₂ cup milk
¹/₃ cup grated Cheddar cheese

Steam the cauliflower and carrot for 6 minutes, then add the peas and zucchini and cook for a further 4 minutes.

Meanwhile make the cheese sauce in the usual way (see page 59). Mash, chop or purée the vegetables with the sauce.

Green Fingers

Green beans make great finger food. To make them more appealing arrange them in a pattern on the plate.

MAKES 5 PORTIONS

¹/₂ small onion, finely chopped
a little margarine or oil
6 oz green beans, trimmed

1 tablespoon flour
¹/₄ cup chicken broth
¹/₄ cup milk
2 tablespoons grated Swiss cheese

Sauté the onion in a little margarine for about 4 minutes until soft but not golden. Meanwhile steam the beans for 6–8 minutes until tender. Make a sauce with 1 tablespoon margarine, the flour, broth, milk and cheese (page 59). Pour the sauce over the beans and onions or chop coarsely.

FISH

Flounder with Herbs

Easy to make and all the flavor is sealed in a parcel.

MAKES 3 PORTIONS

1 fillet of flounder
1 teaspoon olive oil
1 small tomato, skinned, seeded and
chopped
1 small zucchini, washed and sliced

2 teaspoons chopped chives
1 sprig each of parsley, tarragon and
chervil (optional)

Place the fish fillet on a piece of oiled aluminum foil. Mix all the remaining ingredients together and place on top of the fish. Wrap up securely. Cook in the oven preheated to 350°F for about 12 minutes or until the fish just flakes with a fork. Remove the herb sprigs and mash with a fork.

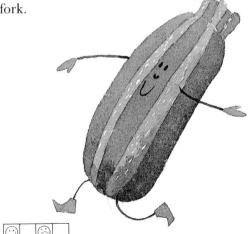

Fingers of Sole

These fingers of sole are fun for babies and toddlers to eat, and make great finger food. They can be served plain or, for older children, with a home-made tomato sauce. Simply purée 3 skinned and seeded tomatoes with a sautéed shallot, 1 tablespoon tomato paste, 2 teaspoons of milk and a teaspoon of finely chopped basil. These 'fish fingers' are much better for your child than commercial ones which are full of coloring and additives. If you are not using all the fingers at once, it is best to freeze them before they are cooked. You can then take out as many fingers as you need for a freshly cooked meal. You could substitute flounder for sole. Crushed cornflakes also make a delicious coating for other types of fish like haddock or cod.

MAKES 8 PORTIONS

1 shallot, peeled and finely chopped
1 tablespoon milk
1 tablespoon vegetable oil
1 sole, filleted and skinned

1 egg
plain flour
crushed cornflakes
a little butter or margarine for frying

Mix together the chopped shallot, half the milk and the oil. Marinate the fish fillets in this mixture for 1 hour. Remove the fillets from the marinade. Cut them into four or five diagonal strips, depending on the size of the sole. Beat the egg together with the remaining milk. Dip the strips first into the flour, then the egg and milk and finally the crushed cornflakes. Fry the fingers in butter until golden brown on both sides. They should take no more than 5 minutes to cook.

Fillets of Sole with Grapes

Fruit and fish mix very well together and the sweetness of the grapes in this recipe gives the sole a delicious taste that babies love. Flounder could be used in place of sole.

MAKES 4 PORTIONS

2 fillets of sole
1 small shallot, peeled and finely chopped

1 teaspoon chopped parsley
⅝ cup milk
1 tablespoon margarine
2 tablespoons all-purpose flour
6 grapes, skinned, halved and seeded

Put the fillets of sole in a dish together with the shallot, and parsley, and pour over the milk. Cook in an oven preheated to 350°F for 8–10 minutes or cover with a lid and microwave on High for 3½ minutes. Once the fish is cooked, drain off and reserve the milk.

Use the margarine, the flour and the flavored milk to make a thick sauce in the usual way (see page 59). Chop the grapes into the sauce. Chop the fish into pieces and pour the sauce over the fish.

Haddock with Vegetables in a Cheese Sauce

Babies love bright colors and the yellow of the corn with the red and green of the pepper and leek makes this dish look attractive. Be careful not to overcook the fish or it will become dry. Once cooked, the fish will just flake with a fork and, mixed with the cheese sauce, will be nice and soft for your baby to eat.

MAKES 6 PORTIONS

6 oz fillet of haddock, skinned
a little margarine
a squeeze of lemon (optional)
¼ cup leek, washed and shredded
¼ cup frozen corn
¼ red bell pepper, skinned, seeded and chopped

Cheese sauce
1 tablespoon margarine
2 teaspoons all-purpose flour
¾ cup milk
¼ cup grated Cheddar cheese

Put the fish into a dish, dot with margarine and add a squeeze of lemon juice, if using. Cover with a lid and microwave for 4 minutes on High. Alternately cook the fish in an oven preheated to 350°F for 8–10 minutes.

Sauté the leek in a little margarine for 2 minutes. Cook the corn and pepper in boiling water until tender (about 6 minutes). Make the cheese sauce in the usual way (see page 59). Flake the fish with a fork and stir it, the vegetables and pepper into the cheese sauce.

Salmon with a Creamy Chive Sauce

Salmon is easy to cook. It can be cooked very quickly in the microwave but here I have wrapped it in aluminum foil with some vegetables and herbs and cooked it more slowly to bring out the flavor.

MAKES 5 PORTIONS

4 oz fillet of salmon
2 teaspoons lemon juice
$^1/_2$ small onion, peeled and sliced
$^1/_2$ bay leaf
1 button mushroom, washed and sliced
$^1/_2$ small tomato, cut into chunks
a sprig of parsley
a little butter

Chive sauce
$^1/_2$ tablespoon margarine
2 teaspoons all-purpose flour
$^5/_8$ cup milk
cooking liquid from the fish
2 teaspoons snipped chives

Wrap the salmon in aluminum foil with the rest of the ingredients and bake in an oven preheated to 325°F for 20 minutes. Meanwhile, make a thick white sauce, using the margarine, flour and milk in the usual way (see page 59).

Once the salmon is cooked, remove it from the foil, strain off the cooking liquid and add this to the white sauce. Finally, stir the chopped chives into the sauce. Flake the salmon and pour the chive sauce over it.

☺ ☹

97

CHICKEN

Chicken with Apple

The sweetness of the apple makes this chicken recipe especially appealing to babies.

MAKES 4 PORTIONS

1 apple, peeled, cored and sliced
1 small cooked single chicken breast, chopped

a little margarine
a squeeze of lemon juice

Cook the apple in a saucepan over a low heat with a little water until soft. Mix the chicken together with the mashed apple. Add the margarine and lemon juice.

Chicken and Apple Balls

This is a tasty recipe, very easy to make and the apple blends really well with the chicken to bring out the flavor and keep it moist. These little balls make great finger food.

MAKES 10 GOLF-BALLS

3 single breasts of chicken or 6 thighs, off the bone and skinned
1 large dessert apple, peeled
1 tablespoon lemon juice
1/2 small onion, peeled and finely chopped

1 tablespoon chopped fresh thyme or parsley
1 small egg, beaten
pinch mixed dried herbs
all-purpose flour
vegetable oil

Chop the chicken very finely in the food processor and grate the apple. Mix the lemon juice with the apple to stop it turning brown. Combine the chicken, apple, onion, herbs and beaten egg. Mix well together and season with a pinch of mixed herbs. Form into little balls and roll in flour. Heat oil in a frying pan and when it is really hot, shallow-fry the balls until they are golden and cooked through (about 6 minutes). ☺ ☹

Bang Bang Chicken

So called because my son likes to help when I flatten the chicken by banging it with a mallet! You can prepare these chicken fingers in advance. Before frying the chicken, cut it into strips, wrap each strip separately and freeze. Just take one or two strips out of the freezer and fry them for freshly cooked chicken.

MAKES 8 PORTIONS

1 double chicken breast, skinned and off the bone
3 slices wholewheat bread
1 tablespoon grated Parmesan cheese (optional)
1 tablespoon chopped parsley (optional)
2 tablespoons all-purpose flour
1 egg, beaten
vegetable oil

Cover the chicken with waxed paper and flatten with a mallet or rolling pin. Make bread crumbs from the slices of bread in a food processor. If you are using the Parmesan and parsley, mix these together with the bread crumbs in a bowl.

Dip the chicken into the flour, then into the egg and then finally into the bread crumbs. Fry in oil for 3–4 minutes each side until golden on the outside and cooked through. Drain well. Cool. Cut the chicken breasts into strips and let your baby hold them as he eats.

Creamy Chicken with Spinach

For young babies this makes a nice creamy purée. For toddlers, chop the chicken, serve it on a bed of spinach and pour over the sauce.

MAKES 3 PORTIONS

1 single chicken breast, skinned and boneless
vegetable oil
³/₄ cup Creamy Pasta Sauce (see page 68)

2 cups spinach, chopped
2 tablespoons grated Parmesan cheese
¹/₄ teaspoon grated nutmeg

Sauté the chicken in a little oil until cooked through. Make the pasta sauce (see page 68). Cook the spinach in boiling water for 4 minutes. Drain and press out all the water. Stir in the Parmesan and nutmeg. Combine the chicken, pasta sauce and spinach and chop in a food processor.

☺ ☹

Chicken with Summer Vegetables

In the summer, you can often find different varieties of squash – some are round, some green and some yellow. They are all delicious, but this recipe can also be made simply with zucchini.

MAKES 3 PORTIONS

1 single chicken breast, on the bone and skinned
vegetable oil
¹/₂ cup chicken broth (see page 62)
2 zucchini, washed and finely chopped

¹/₄ red bell pepper, seeded and finely chopped
1 shallot, peeled and finely chopped
a small piece of yellow squash, finely chopped
¹/₂ tablespoon chopped basil

Fry the chicken breast in a little oil for about 5 minutes. Pour the chicken broth over and simmer for 10 minutes. Add the finely chopped vegetables and basil, cover and simmer for a further 10 minutes.

Remove the chicken from the bone, cut flesh into very small pieces and serve it with the vegetables and chicken broth. If necessary you can make it into a rough purée in a blender or food processor.

Chicken with Cornflakes

Cornflakes are very versatile, and I often use them instead of bread crumbs to coat both chicken and fish.

MAKES 6 PORTIONS

1 egg, beaten
2 tablespoons milk
2 cups cornflakes, crushed

1 double chicken breast, skinned and off the bone
2 tablespoons margarine, melted

Mix together the beaten egg and milk in a shallow dish. In a separate dish, spread out the cornflake crumbs. Dip the chicken breast first into the egg and then coat with the cornflakes. Put the chicken into a greased ovenproof dish and pour over the melted margarine. Bake for about 1 hour in the oven preheated to 350°F.

Chicken with Winter Vegetables

This is quick and easy to prepare and has a delicious rich chicken flavor. It is good with mashed potato.

MAKES 6 PORTIONS

1 double chicken breast, on the bone and skinned
a little flour
vegetable oil
1 small onion, peeled and finely chopped

1 white of leek, washed and sliced
1 carrot, peeled and sliced
1 celery stalk, trimmed and sliced
1¼ cups chicken broth (see page 62)

Cut the chicken breast into four pieces, roll each in flour and brown them in a little oil for 3–4 minutes. In another frying pan, sauté the onion and leek in a little oil for 5 minutes until soft and golden. Put the chicken into a casserole together with all the vegetables and the broth. Cook in an oven preheated to 350°F for 1 hour, stirring half-way through.

Take the chicken off the bone and chop it into little pieces with the vegetables or purée it together with the cooking liquid in a mill or blender.

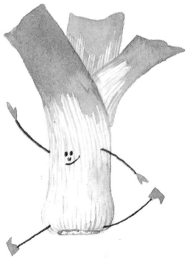

RED MEATS

Beef Casserole with Carrots

This recipe has a delicious rich taste. The secret is to cook the meat for a long time so that it is very tender and has a good flavor from the onions and carrots.

MAKES 8 PORTIONS

2 medium onions, peeled and sliced
vegetable oil
12 oz lean stewing beef, trimmed and cut into small chunks
2 medium carrots, peeled and sliced

1 beef bouillon cube, crumbled
1 tablespoon chopped parsley
1½ cups water
2 large potatoes, peeled and cut into quarters

Fry the onion till golden in a little oil, then add the meat chunks and brown. Transfer the meat and onions to a small casserole and add all the rest of the ingredients except for the potatoes. Cook, covered, in an oven preheated to 350°F for 30 minutes, then turn down the heat and cook for a further 3½ hours at 325°F. One hour before you finish cooking the meat, add the potato.

Chop the meat quite finely in a food processor or blender so that it is easy for your baby to chew. If the meat gets too dry during cooking, add a little extra water. For older children, you can also add mushrooms and tomatoes to this recipe half an hour before the end of cooking time.

Liver Casserole

I have found that mothers who do not like liver themselves seldom cook it for their children. But liver is very good for children; it is easy to digest, a good source of iron and is also very easy to cook. I must admit that I dislike the taste of liver having been forced to eat it as a child at school but, to my great surprise, my one-year-old son adored it. This recipe is good served with mashed potato.

MAKES 8 PORTIONS

1 small onion, peeled and chopped
vegetable oil
1 large or 2 small carrots, peeled and chopped
8 oz calf's liver, trimmed and sliced

1 tomato, skinned, seeded and chopped
1 tablespoon vegetable broth (see page 33)
2 teaspoons chopped parsley

Fry the onion in a little oil until transparent. Add the chopped carrot and continue to fry for about 4 minutes. Add the liver, tomato, broth and parsley. Simmer over a low heat for 15–20 minutes. Cut the liver into small pieces or blend for a few seconds to make a rough purée.

Savory Veal Casserole

A delicious casserole of veal, vegetables and fresh herbs – just increase the quantities for a meal the whole family can enjoy.

MAKES 3 PORTIONS

1 small onion, peeled and finely chopped
1 carrot, scraped and sliced
1/2 stick celery, sliced
vegetable oil

4 oz lean veal for stewing
1 sprig rosemary
1 sprig parsley
1/2 cup water

F ry the onion, carrot and celery in a little oil for 3 minutes. Cut the veal into chunks and put it into a saucepan with the vegetables, herbs and the water. Simmer slowly, covered for 1 hour, (stirring once). Remove the herbs and roughly chop the veal and vegetables in a food processor

☺ | ☹

Special Steak

This recipe makes a very good introduction to red meat for your baby. Later you could merely chop the steak (fillet or rump) in the food processor so that it is easy to chew and more palatable for your baby. You could also leave out the potato.

MAKES 3 PORTIONS

1 medium potato, peeled
2 tablespoons margarine
1 shallot or onion, peeled and finely chopped
2 oz fillet steak

1 small zucchini, washed and chopped
¹/₄ red bell pepper, skinned, seeded and chopped
2 tablespoons milk

B oil the potato until soft. Melt the margarine and sauté the chopped shallot, zucchini and red bell pepper. Top the steak with the chopped shallot and vegetable mixture. Cook on foil under the broiler for 3 minutes each side. Mash the potato together with the milk then purée in a blender together with the steak. Put through a mill if you want to make a very smooth purée.

Creamy Beef Hash

For babies who are good at chewing you could just chop this briefly in a food processor. It is worth buying good quality ground beef as it is leaner and likely to be more tender when cooked.

MAKES 4 PORTIONS

¼ onion, peeled and finely chopped
1 small piece of garlic, finely chopped (optional)
cooking oil
¼ green bell pepper, seeded and finely chopped
4 oz lean ground beef

1 teaspoon each of chopped parsley and basil
1 medium potato, peeled
2 tablespoons milk

Fry the onion and garlic in a little oil for about 5 minutes until soft. Add the green pepper and fry for a further 3 minutes. Add the meat, parsley and basil and cook the meat, stirring, until it turns brown. Add 2 tablespoons water, cover and simmer for 15–20 minutes until the meat is very tender.

Meanwhile, cook the potato until tender and mash together with the milk. Put the potato and meat through a mill to make a very smooth purée.

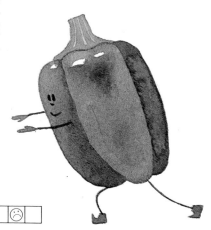

Tasty Rice with Meat and Vegetables

MAKES 8 PORTIONS

¹/₂ onion, peeled and finely chopped
1 carrot, scrubbed and finely chopped
vegetable oil
8 oz lean ground beef
¹/₂ tablespoon tomato catsup
a few drops of Worcestershire sauce

Rice
¹/₃ cup brown rice
2 cups chicken broth (see page 62)
¹/₂ red bell pepper, seeded and finely chopped
¹/₂ cup peas, fresh or frozen

Put the rice into a saucepan and cover with the chicken broth. Bring to a boil and simmer for 15 minutes. Add the red pepper and peas and cook for a further 5 minutes.

Meanwhile sauté the onion and carrot in a little vegetable oil for 3 minutes. Add the ground meat and cook, stirring, until browned. Stir in the tomato catsup and Worcestershire sauce and cook over a gentle heat for 10 minutes. Chop the meat in a food processor for about 30 seconds to make it easier for your baby to chew.

Put the meat into a saucepan, stir in the rice (with the chicken broth) and cook over a gentle heat for 3–4 minutes.

PASTA

Salmon and Vegetable Tagliatelle

Pasta combines with fish well – use canned or fresh salmon.

MAKES 8 PORTIONS OF SAUCE

1 small carrot
$^1/_2$ cup broccoli flowerets
$^1/_2$ cup snow peas trimmed and cut
into strips
$^1/_2$ cup corn
4 oz canned salmon, drained

Cheese Sauce
1 tablespoon butter or margarine
1 tablespoon flour
$^1/_2$ teaspoon dried mustard
1 cup milk
$^1/_2$ cup grated Cheddar cheese
$^1/_2$ tablespoon chopped parsley
1 tablespoon freshly grated Parmesan

Cut the carrot into small strips. Steam with the broccoli and snow peas until tender crisp. Add the corn and cook for the last 3 minutes. Make the cheese sauce in the usual way (see page 59). Add the vegetables and salmon, mix with cooked tagliatelle and sprinkle with parmesan. Chop finely or coarsely.

Bolognese Sauce with Eggplant

Spaghetti ($^1/_2$–$^3/_4$ cup cooked, $^1/_4$–$^3/_8$ cup dry per serving) is a firm favorite with older babies and toddlers.

MAKES 12 PORTIONS OF SAUCE

1 eggplant, peeled and sliced
salt
1 medium onion, finely chopped
1/4 garlic clove, finely chopped
vegetable oil
1 small green bell, pepper, finely
chopped

1 lb lean ground meat
1 tablespoon tomato paste
1/4 teaspoon oregano
1 cup chicken broth (see page 62)
dash of Worcestershire sauce

Sprinkle the eggplant with a little salt and leave to drain for 30 minutes. Rinse well and pat dry. Sauté the onion and garlic in a little oil for 3 minutes. Add the green pepper and cook for a further 3 minutes. Stir in the meat and cook until browned. Add the tomato paste, herbs, and broth. Bring to a boil and simmer for 25 minutes. Fry the eggplant slices in a little oil until golden. Pat dry with kitchen paper. Chop in the food processor with the cooked meat for about 45 seconds.

Chicken Pasta Sauce

Serve with tagliatelle (1/2–3/4 cup cooked pasta per serving).

MAKES 3 PORTIONS OF SAUCE

1 single boneless chicken breast,
skinned
a little margarine, melted

2 inches white of leek, sliced
1 tomato, skinned, seeded and
chopped

Baste the chicken breast with a little melted margarine and broil for 20 minutes or sauté the chicken for about 10 minutes.
Sauté the leek in a little margarine for 5 minutes. Add the chopped tomato and continue to cook for 2–3 minutes. Chop the chicken finely and combine it with the vegetables and cooked pasta or purée if necessary.

Baked Pasta with Vegetables

This is good vegetable pasta recipe for the whole family. My one-year-old daughter always goes straight for the broccoli. I think it must be the bright green color that she likes.

MAKES 10 PORTIONS

1 cup pasta spirals
1 cup each broccoli and cauliflower
flowerets
1/3 cup corn
4 button mushrooms, sliced
a little margarine
10 oz can condensed cream of chicken
soup

1 tablespoon cornstarch
1 tablespoon heavy cream
1 tablespoon chopped chives
2 slices wholewheat toast made into
bread crumbs
1/4 cup grated Parmesan cheese

Cook the pasta according to packet directions. Drain and put into an ovenproof dish. Steam the broccoli and cauliflower for 6 minutes and add the corn halfway through. Sauté the mushrooms in a little margarine for 3–4 minutes. Add all the vegetables to the pasta in the dish. Heat the soup in saucepan. Mix a little of the soup with the cornstarch and mix into the rest of the soup in the pan. Stir over a low heat to thicken. Add the cream and chives and pour over the cooked pasta and vegetables in the dish. Sprinkle with bread crumbs and Parmesan and dot with margarine. Bake in an oven preheated to 350°F for 10–15 minutes. Run under a hot broiler for 5 minutes to make a crispy topping. Chop as needed.

Pasta Shell Salad

This can be made with all sorts of different pasta – animal-shaped pasta is fun if you can find it! You can vary the basic recipe by adding different vegetables like corn or red bell pepper. Toast the sesame seeds in a dry frying pan until golden.

MAKES 3 PORTIONS

CHICKEN SALAD	FISH SALAD
1 single cooked chicken breast, chopped	4–6 oz can tuna, or salmon, drained
1 tomato, skinned, seeded and chopped	2 tablespoons salad cream or mayonnaise
1/4 cucumber, chopped	1/2 cup corn
2 teaspoons mayonnaise	1 tomato, skinned, seeded and chopped
2 teaspoons cottage cheese	1 scallion, very finely chopped
1 teaspoon tomato catsup	1/3 cup cooked pasta shells
1/3 cup cooked pasta shells	2 tablespoons toasted sesame seeds
1 tablespoon toasted sesame seeds	

Choose chicken or fish salad. Mix all the ingredients together except for the sesame seeds which you sprinkle over the top.

NINE TO TWELVE MONTH MEAL PLANNER

	Breakfast	*Sleep*	*Lun*
Day 1	Fruity Swiss Muesli Yogurt with Dried Fruit Milk	Milk	Chicken and Finger ve Strawberry Ju
Day 2	Chex (or other cereal) Cheese on toast Fruit Milk	Milk	Special Fruit C Ju
Day 3	Scrambled egg and toast Fruit with cottage cheese Milk	Milk	Fillets of Sole Baked Apples Ju
Day 4	Cheese and Raisin Delight Cheerios (or other cereal) Fruit Milk	Milk	Liver C Multi-Colore Papaya Ju
Day 5	French Toast Fruit Compote Milk	Milk	Bang Ban Cabbage Fruit C Jui
Day 6	Fruity Swiss Muesli Yogurt and Dried Fruit Milk	Milk	Beef Casse Car Baked B Jui
Day 7	Cheese Scramble Fruity Yogurt Milk	Milk	Chicken wi Veget Fresh Pear wi Jui

Early Supper	Dinner	Bedtime
Cabbage Surprise Fruit Milk	Miniature sandwiches Finger vegetables Juice	Milk
Creamy Eggplant Pasta Zucchini Purée with Cottage Cheese Milk	Fruit with Ricotta Rusk Juice	Milk
Pasta and vegetables with Creamy Pasta Sauce Fruit and Yogurt Gelatin Milk	Leek and Potato Purée Fruit Juice	Milk
Flounder with Herbs Apple and Blackberry Milk	Finger vegetables with dip Yogurt Juice	Milk
Fingers of Sole, cooked vegetables as finger food Strawberry Rice Pudding Milk	Vegetables in Cheese Sauce Fruit Juice	Milk
Popeye Pasta Apple Purée Milk	Gratin of Carrots Fruit and Yogurt Gelatin Juice	Milk
Lentil and Vegetable Purée Cheese Fruit Milk	Baked Pasta with Vegetables Apple Purée Rusk; Juice	Milk

CHAPTER FIVE

TODDLERS

I find that beyond the age of one, toddlers prefer to exercise their independence and feed themselves. Let your toddler experiment using a spoon and fork – you never know, some food might find its way into his mouth! A handy tip is to put a clean towel or some kitchen paper under your toddler's high chair to catch the food that gets dropped over the side; this will make sure the food is still clean and can be given back to your child. A 'Pelican' bib – a strong plastic bib which has a tray at the bottom to catch stray food – is also good. If your toddler has difficulty eating with a spoon, try giving him finger foods like goujons of fish or raw vegetables with a dip. You must still be careful, though, to keep food like olives, nuts or fresh litchis out of the reach of young children. Toddlers love to put everything in their mouths and it would be so easy for them to choke on such foods.

Toddlers, unlike adults, do not have strict meal times. They are probably more sensible than us and will eat when they are hungry and no amount of coaxing will get them to eat when they are not. Many toddlers prefer lots of small meals during the day to three main meals. In fact doctors have proved that this is a healthier way of eating. There is plenty of time when he grows older and when he goes to school to establish a regular meal pattern. There is a whole section in this book on healthy snacks, so don't make the mistake of giving your toddler sweets or processed snacks when he could enjoy eating a dip with a bowl of raw vegetables much more. Toddlers who get used to eating healthy snacks are more likely to continue the same habits later on in life. However, it would also be wrong to make candy and doughnuts the forbidden fruit, or your toddler would crave them all the more and gorge himself on them whenever he was out of the house.

Many toddlers enjoy eating much more sophisticated food than we would imagine possible. Let your child try food from your plate and you may find yourself very surprised by the tastes he enjoys. Of course food from Mommy's or Daddy's plate is much more interesting than his own meal and you can sometimes entice your child to eat better if you put his meal on your plate. But the point at this stage is that the toddler can now eat, to a large extent, what you adults are eating. I am a great believer in giving toddlers 'grown-up' foods as soon as possible and almost all the recipes following are suitable for the whole family. *Do* eat with your child rather than just sit there shoveling food into his mouth. He'll eat much more happily *with* you – after all, who enjoys eating alone?

Try and reform your own eating habits by adding less salt and sugar to your food and your toddler will be able to enjoy almost everything you cook. Happy meal times together, and I hope your children will introduce you to some great new recipes.

My Child Won't Eat!

After the age of one, your child will be expending much more energy and nearly all toddlers at some stage will lose interest in food and would much rather play with their toys and run around. This can be a very difficult time and it is important not to make a big fuss if your child refuses to eat. He will eat when he is hungry and the more you fuss the more he will refuse his food. Be patient with him, he will grow out of this phase.

If your toddler really enjoys his food and eats well at meal times, then you really are a lucky mother. I know so many mothers who worry constantly that their child is not eating enough. Most of these worries are unnecessary and toddlers can thrive very well on remarkably little food.

Toddlers are very unpredictable; some days they will be ravenous, and other days they will eat practically nothing. If you judge a child's food intake over a whole week, you won't worry as much if one day he refuses to eat anything.

Many mothers complain that their toddler will not touch meat or fish but there are lots of other equally good sources of protein like peanut butter, eggs or dairy produce. Then there are the mothers who are tearing their hair out because their children will only eat one thing. This is also quite normal; children, unlike adults, like repetition in their diet and they are often wary of trying new foods. Very often, if you let your child choose his own diet, you would be surprised that he might, without any coaxing on your part, choose a balanced one.

There are several ways in which you can try to encourage your child to eat. You might vary the venue of his meals. My son enjoys eating his meals in the play house in the garden. He also loves to have a little party and invite his favorite teddy bears; we lay food on a low table in his playroom, he pretends to feed the bears and then eats the food himself. It is all part of a game and he loves it. Eating becomes fun and is no longer a battle of wills.

Toddlers enjoy playing with food and they are interested in the feel of different foods. It is a good idea sometimes to let your child help prepare his meals; for example, he could help you stir the gelatin or shell the peas. This is all part of a learning process and food should be fun. Let your toddler poke his finger into the gelatin and see it wobble – there is time to teach him table manners once he has finished experimenting. You may well stimulate an interest in food by getting him to 'help' (under supervision, of course). My son is always willing to lend a helping hand, especially when it comes to making cookies; he loves to knead the dough, roll it out and cut it into shapes, much more fun than play dough!

Letting them experiment with different spoons and forks and praising them when they manage to get the food into their mouth is another way to encourage them to eat. We have little Chinese meals at home and I feed them with chopsticks. You should see how they enjoy it and how wide they open their mouths!

A great deal of problem eating can be overcome by attractive presentation. We can learn a lot from the Japanese who believe that food should please the eye as well as the stomach. Color is very important and it is interesting that most toddlers go for the brightly colored foods first. Try to choose contrasting colors to make the food look appealing. It is a good idea to use plastic plates with separate compartments (you can buy these in most supermarkets) and present your toddler with two or three foods in separate sections – keep the dessert out of sight until the main course has been eaten!

Sometimes it is fun to arrange food in a pattern on the plate. You can help teach your child by arranging food in the shape of numbers or letters or make the food into the shape of a face. You can use some small-sized novelty cookie cutters to cut out shapes from bread, sandwiches or cheese to stimulate your child's interest. Another tip is to call food by funny names like Bugs Bunny carrots or Mickey Mouse soup. You may laugh but if your toddler thinks this is what his favorite character eats for lunch, he is more likely to eat it himself!

Never put too much food on a plate – much better that he should ask for more. Toddlers love individual portions of food. Make individual casseroles, for example (much nicer than a dollop of meat and potatoes on a plate) and miniature cakes rather than slices from a large cake.

If you have given your toddler a good choice of foods and he still refuses to eat, it is not then a good idea to offer him the contents of the fridge and pantry. Explain that this is his meal and that there is nothing else on offer. If he is very restless and clearly not interested, just put the food back in the fridge and bring it out a little later. You will be making a rod for your own back otherwise and nine times out of ten he is just not hungry. Adults are conditioned into eating three meals a day but toddlers will only eat when they are hungry – and no child has ever starved to death through stubbornness.

If you make eating fun, then your children will be tucking in with you. Eat as a family as much as possible. An occasional trip to a restaurant does wonders to stimulate a child's appetite. Even going to a friend's house for supper can help sometimes, especially if there is another child present who likes to tuck in!

The Foods to Choose

Now that your child is twelve months old, you can switch from formula to full-fat cow's milk. Do not give him skim milk. Unless he is really obese he will need a diet that contains at least 40 percent fat; and unless obesity runs in your family, the chances are that you do not need to worry about it. A lot of parents nowadays are concerned about their children's cholesterol level and put them on low-fat diets from a very early age but cholesterol guidelines do not apply in the same way to most normal toddlers as they do to adults. Growing children need more dietary fat than adults and should not be given low-fat produce. Fat is a rich source of both the fatty acids and the fat-soluble vitamins needed for a child's growth. Also fat is concentrated calories and provides almost twice as much energy as either proteins or carbohydrates. There are, of course, exceptions to this rule, and an overweight toddler should have his fat intake restricted. In general terms, stick to healthy cooking, cutting fat from meat, and cooking with vegetable fats rather than animal or saturated fats.

Vegetable dishes at this stage can be served to the whole family as a main meal. This is useful if your child goes through a stage of refusing to eat any meat and you need to supplement his diet with protein-rich foods like nuts, beans, legumes and soy products. (It's also vital for children who are being brought up as vegetarians.)

You can now include healthy 'convenience' fish like canned tuna and

salmon which are cheaper than fresh fish. Chicken dishes too can be more versatile – I've tried to make this a fairly international section. Chicken is so low in fat, and such a favorite with us that I'm sure one day my husband will turn into one, the amount he eats!

Although more and more people are turning away from red meat in favor of fish and chicken, you must bear in mind that red meat provides more iron and zinc than either fish or poultry and that you should supplement your child's diet by providing other sources of these minerals – leafy green vegetables, beans and nuts for instance. You could offer your toddler foods like hamburgers and meatballs, so long as the meat is lean – you can ask your butcher to grind some lean cuts especially for you. Do not give your toddler processed meats like sausages, salami or corned beef.

Pasta is still a great favorite with toddlers. There is a wonderful variety available to choose from; you can stuff canneloni, make a tomato sauce for fresh ravioli containing ricotta and spinach, or entice your child to eat meat by making spaghetti bolognese. (My son, Nicholas, who shows little enthusiasm for eating ground meat, will gobble it all up if it is stuffed inside canneloni or served as a spaghetti sauce.) You can even teach your toddler to read by buying alphabet spaghetti! Individual pieces of pasta like penne (tubes) or papardelle (bow-ties) are still much easier for toddlers to eat than long strands of spaghetti. (Although Nicholas, when 20 months, invented his own method of eating spaghetti – he held it out in front of him by the two ends and sucked in from the middle! Not the height of good manners perhaps, but certainly very efficient.)

FRUIT AND DESSERTS

There are many recipes here for cold and cooked desserts which can be enjoyed by the whole family, but there is still nothing more delicious or better for you and your child than fresh ripe fruit. None of the vitamins and nutrients are destroyed through cooking, and it makes great finger food for your toddler. My son adores fruit so much that we have to hide the fruit bowl until he finishes his main course. He would far rather eat fruit than oversweet puddings, cakes and chocolates. Serve fruit on a daily basis and one of these desserts every now and again as a treat.

Present fresh fruit in an attractive way; contrast colors on the plate; cut the fruits into interesting shapes and arrange in patterns. Always make sure that you remove any pits before giving to your toddler – he could so easily choke.

Where raw fruit is concerned, there are endless variations on a theme. Purée or grate fruits and mix them with cottage cheese or yogurt and wheatgerm. Cut the fruit into bite-sized chunks and cover with yogurt and honey or home-made custard sauce. Dried fruits which have been soaked make great finger foods.

Try giving your children some more exotic fruits like Sharon fruit which looks like an orange tomato. It is a variety of persimmon from Israel. It tastes wonderful mashed with cottage cheese and can be found in large supermarkets when it is in season. Kiwi fruit is high in Vitamin C and makes a good snack cut into slices, and mango and papaya blend very well with dairy produce.

Fruits can also be puréed for use in ice creams. Ice creams in all colors, shapes and sizes are sold all over the world.

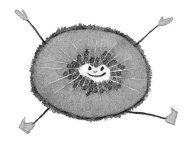

However the quality of some products has nothing to do with the true home-made experience. I think that there is nothing to beat the combination of milk, cream or yogurt and wonderful home-made fruit purées – far better for all of us than ingredients like skim milk, vegetable fat, glucose syrup, whey solids, guar gum, emulsifier stabilisers and artificial flavors that can be found in many commercial ice creams lingering in the deep freezes of supermarkets. In Britain alone, on average $680 million a year is spent on ice cream and there *are* some good commercial ice creams made from natural ingredients only but you do need to look out for them.

If you enjoy making your own ice cream it really is worth investing in a small ice-cream making machine. Believe me, you will put it to good use through the year and your children will be very popular with their friends when they come for supper. If you do not have an ice-cream maker do not be put off making your own home-made ice creams. Just pour the prepared mixture into a plastic container, cover with foil or a plastic bag and place in the freezer until firm (3–4 hours). Break the mixture into pieces, put it into a food processor bowl and beat with a metal blade until light and fluffy but not thawed. This should get rid of the ice particles in the mixture, and for a really smooth texture, it is advisable to repeat this process at least twice during freezing. Put the ice cream back into the freezer in the plastic container. Ice cream tastes best if you take it out of the freezer 10 minutes before you serve it.

Another simple way of serving ice cream is to pour the mixture into molds to make suckers – toddlers love these (see page 171).

BAKING FOR TODDLERS

A toddler's first birthday is a big occasion in his life and probably even more exciting for his parents and grandparents! It is great fun preparing the food for a child's party. Anyone can call a store and order a birthday cake in the shape of a train, but how much more impressive and satisfying it is to bake and decorate your own. Your child will love to help with the mixing and decorating – probably more fun than eating it.

Any basic sponge or fruit cake mixture could be adapted to a novelty shape, if you like. There are many smaller cakes which can be served at a child's party. Many of the baking recipes contain healthy ingredients, cutting out undesirables as much as possible but some are sheer uncompromised treats.

HEALTHY SNACKS

If your toddler is happy to eat three main meals a day, then that is wonderful and very convenient for everyone, but let's face it, nearly all toddlers snack between meals. Whereas for some this just supplements their meal, many toddlers do not have the patience to sit down and eat a proper meal and they get most of their nutrition from snacks during the day. Toddlers' stomachs are small and it is often difficult for them to eat enough at breakfast, say, to last them until lunchtime when they have been rushing around all morning. As I said earlier, lots of small meals – healthy snacks – during the day are in fact healthier than three main meals. Snacks are therefore a very important part of a toddler's diet. If you encourage your child when he is very young to enjoy eating healthy snacks in preference to candy and chips, it is likely that he will continue these habits later in life and enjoy a much healthier diet.

Stock your pantry and fridge with healthful snacks and when you take your toddler out, try to remember to take a small bag of healthy snacks with you. Toddlers expend a lot of energy and it doesn't take them long to get hungry again after a meal.

Textures and Quantities

There is no longer any need to purée your child's food; on the contrary, he should be getting used to chewing. The longer you continue with purées because that is the way your child prefers his food, the more difficult it will become to encourage him to chew and swallow his food properly. In fact chewing on something hard like a raw carrot should help to relieve sore gums. A lot of toddlers, however, do not like to chew chunks of meat, and it is sometimes necessary to break meat down in a blender before serving. I find that ground meat, liver or chicken goes down better with most toddlers than chunks of meat.

Underneath each recipe, I have given quantities in adult portions. Every child is different, and you must judge the portion size on your toddler's appetite. He can eat anything from one-quarter of an adult portion to a whole portion if he is exceptionally hungry and greedy! (If your toddler is becoming overweight, then you should consult your doctor and consider putting him on a low-fat diet.)

VEGETABLES

Ratatouille

Vegetables tend to be quite soft in ratatouille and so are easy for your toddler to chew. Choose firm eggplants and zucchini; if they are not fresh, the ratatouille may taste bitter. For a more substantial meal finish the dish with a cheesy crumb topping.

MAKES 6 ADULT PORTIONS

2 eggplants
salt and pepper to taste
2 onions, peeled and chopped
1/2 clove of garlic, crushed (optional)
olive oil
1 green and 1 red bell pepper, seeded and diced

4 zucchini, trimmed and sliced
2 large tomatoes, skinned, seeded and chopped
1 bay leaf
1 sprig of thyme
1 tablespoon chopped parsley

Cut the eggplants into 1/4-inch slices (do not peel). Put them in a colander, sprinkle with salt and set aside for 30–40 minutes (to drain out bitter flavors). Meanwhile cook the onion and garlic in 2 tablespoons of the oil until the onion is soft and transparent. Add the bell peppers and a little more oil if necessary and cook for a further 3 minutes. Transfer the onions and peppers to a casserole dish.

Rinse the eggplant slices and dry with paper towels. Fry them in very hot olive oil to begin with (to seal the surface), then reduce the heat and fry for a further 5 minutes. Drain. Transfer the eggplant to the casserole dish and add the sliced zucchini, chopped tomato, herbs and seasoning to taste. Cook in an oven preheated to 350°F, covered, for about 30 minutes.

☺ ☹

Ratatouille Crumble

Follow the recipe left for the ratatouille up to the stage of putting into the oven. And instead of a casserole, use a fairly shallow oval dish.

MAKES 8 PORTIONS

Ratatouille (see opposite)

Crumble topping
2 tablespoons margarine
1 cup all-purpose flour

¹/₂ cup finely grated Cheddar cheese
¹/₄ cup freshly grated Parmesan cheese
1 tablespoon finely chopped fresh parsley

For the topping, cut the margarine into the flour until it resembles bread crumbs, then add the cheeses and parsley. Top the ratatouille in the dish with the mixture, and cook in the oven pre-heated to 350°F for 30 minutes. Run under the broiler just before serving.

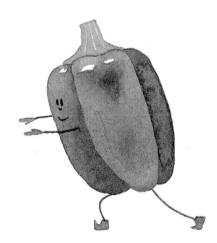

Stuffed Potatoes

Stuffed potatoes make an excellent meal for toddlers and there are endless variations on the fillings you can make. Prick medium potatoes all over and brush with oil. Bake in an oven preheated to 375°F for 1¼–1½ hours, or until tender (or you can bake them in the microwave). Carefully spoon the soft flesh out of the skins leaving enough round the sides so that the skins keep their shape. You are now ready to make the various fillings.

Vegetable and Cheese Potato Filling

MAKES 4 ADULT PORTIONS

¼ cup each of small broccoli and cauliflower flowerets
4 medium baked potatoes
1 tablespoon margarine
½ cup milk

½ cup grated Cheddar cheese
2 medium tomatoes, skinned and cut into small pieces
½ teaspoon salt
grated cheese to finish

Steam the cauliflower and broccoli until they are tender (about 6 minutes), then chop finely. Meanwhile mash the potato flesh with the margarine and milk until smooth and creamy. Mix in the cheese, tomatoes, cooked chopped vegetables and salt and scoop the mixture back into the potato skins. Sprinkle a little extra grated cheese on top and brown under the broiler.

Chicken or Tuna
Potato Filling

MAKES 2 ADULT PORTIONS

1 medium onion, peeled and finely chopped
1 tablespoon cooking oil
²⁄₃ cup button mushrooms, washed and thinly sliced
2 medium baked potatoes

tablespoon margarine
¹⁄₂ cup milk
1 cup cooked chicken breast, chopped, or canned tuna, drained and flaked
2 tablespoons chopped parsley
1 tablespoon tomato catsup

Sauté the onion in the oil until transparent. Add the mushrooms and cook for a further 3 minutes. Mash the potato flesh with the margarine and milk, then combine with all the remaining ingredients. Spoon into the potato skins. Bake for 10 minutes in an oven preheated to 350°F and serve.

Stuffed Tomatoes

Another easy dish, which can be prepared in advance and which looks very appealing.

MAKES 2 ADULT PORTIONS

2 eggs
2 medium tomatoes
1 tablespoon mayonnaise

1 tablespoon snipped chives
salt and pepper

Hard-boil both the eggs. Meanwhile skin the tomatoes, then cut the tops off and scoop out the inside. Discard the seeds but keep the tiny bits of flesh. When the eggs are ready, peel and mash them together with the pieces of tomato, mayonnaise, chives and a little salt and pepper. Stuff into the tomatoes and replace the tomato tops on the egg mixture.

☺ ☹

Tasty Peanut Rissoles

Combining vegetables with nuts makes a good high-protein meal for your toddler and this is a delicious combination which the rest of the family will enjoy too!

MAKES 8 RISSOLES

1 onion, peeled and finely chopped
1 celery stalk, diced
1 carrot, scraped and diced
vegetable oil
1/2 red bell pepper, seeded and diced
2/3 cup mushrooms, washed and diced

1/2 cup green beans
1/4 cup unsalted roasted peanuts
1/3 cup cooked brown rice
1 egg, beaten
salt and freshly ground pepper
3 slices brown bread made into bread crumbs

Fry the onion, celery and carrot in a little oil for 3 minutes, then add the red pepper and mushrooms and continue to fry until soft. Drain off any excess fat.

Meanwhile steam the green beans until tender, about 8–10 minutes. Chop the nuts and beans in a food processor and add these to the rest of the cooked vegetables along with the rice. Stir in the beaten egg, a little seasoning and a third of the bread crumbs and mix well.

Form the mixture into flat round rissoles and roll them in the remaining bread crumbs. Put the rissoles in the fridge to harden for 1 hour. When you are ready to eat, shallow-fry the rissoles in hot oil.

Potato, Zucchini and Cheese Fritters

These crispy vegetable fritters have a delicious taste.

MAKES 4 ADULT PORTIONS

2 medium potatoes, peeled
2 medium zucchini, trimmed
1/2 cup grated Cheddar cheese
2 eggs, lightly beaten

a pinch of ground nutmeg
salt and pepper to taste
2 tablespoons vegetable oil
2 tablespoons margarine

Coarsely grate the potatoes and zucchini then get rid of as much of their liquid as possible by squeezing them between two plates. Put the vegetables in a bowl and add the grated cheese, eggs and seasonings.

Heat the oil and margarine in a frying pan. Form the vegetable mixture into round, flat cakes and cook over a medium heat, turning frequently to brown both sides.

Spanish Omelet

This is good served cold and cut into wedges the next day. I give suggestions on the right for additions to the basic omelet.

MAKES 6 ADULT PORTIONS

2 medium potatoes, peeled and diced
cooking or olive oil
1 onion, peeled and finely chopped
3 tablespoons chopped green and red bell pepper
²/₃ cup button mushrooms, washed and sliced
1 tablespoon chopped parsley
1 tablespoon grated Parmesan cheese
salt and pepper
4 eggs

Suggested variations
1 tablespoon grated Swiss cheese
OR
1 large chopped tomato
1 tablespoon tomato catsup
OR
¹/₃ cup peas
1 tablespoon snipped chives
OR
¹/₃ cup canned drained tuna
1 cup drained canned chopped tomato
OR
²/₃ cup cooked ham or bacon, cubed

Fry the diced potato in a little oil until brown. Drain well. Fry the onion. After a few minutes, add the peppers. When the onions have turned golden brown, add the mushroom and parsley and cook, stirring over a medium heat, for about 3 minutes. In a bowl, combine the onion mixture with the potatoes, Parmesan, any variation ingredients and season to taste. Beat the eggs and pour them over the vegetable mixture. Heat 2 tablespoons of oil in a frying pan and tip the pan to coat half-way up the sides. Fry the egg mixture for about 8–10 minutes (or until the omelet is lightly browned underneath). To finish, brown under a hot broiler for about 3 minutes. Cut into wedges. Serve either hot or cold.

Vegetarian Rissoles

These rissoles can be eaten hot or cold. They make a great meal for the whole family served with a fresh salad. They freeze very well. It is best to freeze them just after they are rolled in bread crumbs; then you can fry them just before serving.

MAKES 8 RISSOLES

1 onion, peeled and finely chopped
1/3 cup white of leek, chopped
vegetable oil
1 1/2 cups cauliflower flowerets
2 cups shredded cabbage
1 1/4 cups zucchini, trimmed and sliced
salt and pepper to taste

3 cups mushrooms, washed and finely chopped
a squeeze of lemon juice
1/2 cup all-purpose flour
2 teaspoons Vegemite, melted in 1/4 cup hot water
6 slices wholewheat or cracked wheat bread, made into bread crumbs
1 egg, beaten

Fry the chopped onion and leek in a little oil until transparent. Cook the cauliflower, cabbage and zucchini until tender (preferably in a steamer) with a little salt to taste. When the onions are cooked, stir in the chopped mushrooms and cook for a further 3 minutes. Add the lemon juice. Roughly chop the cooked cauliflower, cabbage and zucchini and add to the mushrooms and onions. Stir in the flour and mix well. Stir in the Vegemite water and a little salt and pepper to taste. Stir in a few of the bread crumbs to thicken the mixture, and make into small rissoles with floured hands. (It is best to leave the mixture to cool down first!) Dip the rissoles into beaten egg, a little extra flour and then into the bread crumbs. Chill for 30 minutes to firm up before cooking. Fry in hot oil until golden and crisp on both sides.

☺ ☹

Vegetable Salad with Raspberry Vinegar

This is a refreshing salad for a summer's lunch. The dressing complements the nutty flavor of the corn and adds a little sweetness to the salad.

MAKES 4 ADULT PORTIONS

1 cup cauliflower flowerets
1 cup sliced green beans
1 cup frozen corn
sugar to taste
¼ small lettuce, shredded

8 cherry tomatoes, cut in half
1 hard-boiled egg, grated

Dressing
1 tablespoon raspberry vinegar
2 tablespoons hazelnut oil
salt and pepper to taste

Steam the cauliflower and beans until tender (about 15 minutes). Cook the frozen corn for about 4 minutes in boiling water with a little sugar and salt. When the cauliflower, beans and corn have cooled, put all the salad ingredients in a bowl with the grated egg sprinkled on top. Mix the dressing together with a fork and pour it over the salad.

☺ ☹

Spinach with Sesame Sauce

This dish originates from Japan. It is very nutritious, simple to prepare and delicious. In Japanese restaurants, it is served cold, but it can also be served hot.

MAKES 2 ADULT PORTIONS

4 tablespoons sesame seeds
4 cups spinach, carefully washed and tough stalks removed

1 tablespoon soy sauce
1 teaspoon sugar
3 tablespoons water

Sprinkle the sesame seeds into a dry frying pan and heat, shaking constantly until a pale golden. Meanwhile cook the spinach in a small amount of water for about 5 minutes. When the spinach is cooked press out any water by squeezing between two plates. Crush the seeds in a mill (reserving a few to sprinkle over the spinach) and they will become a fine powder. Mix the powder with the soy sauce, sugar and water until it has the consistency of cream. Roughly chop the spinach, pour over the sesame sauce and sprinkle with the toasted whole sesame seeds.

Special Fried Rice

Babies love rice and this is very appealing as it is so colorful. For older children you can make little sailing boats. Cut a cooked red bell pepper in half, stuff each half with rice and stick two corn chips upright in the rice to look like sails.

MAKES 6 ADULT PORTIONS

1¼ cups basmati rice
¾ cup carrots, washed, scrubbed and diced
2 tablespoons butter
1 cup frozen peas

¾ cup red or yellow bell pepper, washed and diced
2 tablespoons sesame oil
2 chopped hard-boiled eggs

Cook the rice for 15 to 20 minutes until soft. Sauté the carrot in margarine for 3 minutes, then add the peas and peppers and cook for 3 minutes more. Heat the sesame oil in a frying pan, fry the rice in the oil for 2 to 3 minutes. Add the vegetables and chopped egg.

FISH

Grandma's Gefilte Fish

This is my mother's traditional recipe. It is very appealing to children because of the slightly sweet taste of the balls. My son, Nicholas, loves them and they are very easy for him to hold and eat himself. Adults can eat them with horseradish sauce.

MAKES ABOUT 20 BALLS

1 lb minced fish fillet (mix any of the following: haddock, halibut, whitefish, cod or flounder)
1 egg, beaten

1 onion, peeled and chopped very finely in the food processor
1 tablespoon sugar
salt and pepper to taste
light cooking oil

Mix all the ingredients well (except for the oil), and shape into golf-ball-sized balls. Fry carefully until golden brown all over. Drain on paper towels. Serve hot or cold.

Boiled Minced Fish Balls

These are best served cold.

MAKES 20 BALLS

1 lb minced fish (see previous page)
1 egg, beaten
1 carrot, peeled and grated
1 tablespoon chopped parsley
1 onion, peeled and chopped very
finely in the food processor
salt and pepper to taste
1 tablespoon sugar

Fish broth
Some fish bones
1 medium onion, peeled and sliced
2 carrots, scraped and sliced
1 bay leaf
sprig of parsley
4 peppercorns
a little sugar

For the broth, put the fish bones, onion, carrots, bay leaf, parsley, peppercorns, a little salt and a little sugar into a saucepan with 2 pints water. Bring to a boil, skim, and then simmer for 1 hour. Remove the fish bones from the broth.

Mix all the ingredients for the fish balls together. Form into small balls using wet hands. Place the fish into the boiling broth and simmer for about 1 hour.

☺	☹

Nursery Fish Pie

A good, old-fashioned favorite.

MAKES 3 ADULT PORTIONS

12 oz cod fillet
⅝ cup milk
½ bay leaf
salt and pepper (optional)
2 tablespoons margarine
2 tablespoons all-purpose flour
2 tablespoons grated Cheddar cheese
1 tablespoon chopped parsley
1 hard-boiled egg, chopped
a squeeze of lemon juice

Topping
2 medium potatoes, peeled and cut
into pieces
1 tablespoon milk
1 tablespoon margarine

Cut the fish into pieces, put into a saucepan with the milk, bay leaf and a little light seasoning. Bring to a boil, then simmer, uncovered, for about 10 minutes. While the fish is cooking, cook the potato for the topping in boiling salted water until soft. Drain well, mash with the milk and margarine and lightly season.

Drain the fish, reserving the cooking liquid and carefully remove any skin and bones. Melt half the margarine in a heavy-bottomed saucepan and add the flour. Cook gently for 1 minute, then add the fish liquid gradually, then bring to a boil stirring. Simmer the sauce for 3–4 minutes, stirring continuously until smooth. Take off the heat, add the grated cheese and continue to stir until it has completely melted. Fold in the fish, parsley and boiled egg. Add a little seasoning and a squeeze of lemon. Place the fish in a greased serving dish and top with the mashed potato. Bake in an oven preheated to 350°F for 15–20 minutes then dot with the remaining margarine and broil for about 2 minutes until brown and crispy.

Fish in Creamy Mushroom Sauce

For older children, cook 4 cups fresh spinach and lay each whole fillet on a bed of spinach and pour over the sauce.

MAKES 4 ADULT PORTIONS

1 small onion, peeled and finely chopped
2 tablespoons margarine
3 cups button mushrooms, washed and finely chopped

2 tablespoons lemon juice
2 tablespoons chopped parsley
2 tablespoons all-purpose flour
1¼ cups milk
1 sole (or flounder), filleted

Fry the onion in half the margarine until transparent. Add the mushrooms, lemon juice and parsley and cook for 2 minutes. Add the flour and cook for 2 minutes, stirring constantly. Add the milk gradually and cook stirring constantly until the sauce is thick and smooth.

Fry the sole fillets in the rest of the margarine for 2–3 minutes on each side. Cut or flake the fish into small pieces and mix with the mushroom sauce. Alternately, cover the fish with the mushroom sauce and bake in the oven preheated to 350°F for about 15 minutes or until the fish just flakes.

☺	☹	

Gratin of Sole

A very tasty fish recipe which is so easy to make.

MAKES 4 ADULT PORTIONS

4 fillets of sole or flounder
salt and pepper to taste
½ small lemon
1 cup wholewheat bread crumbs

½ cup grated Cheddar cheese
1 heaped tablespoon chopped parsley
¼ cup margarine, melted

Lay the fillets in a greased ovenproof dish and season with salt, pepper and lemon juice. Put the bread crumbs, cheese and parsley in a bowl and stir in the melted margarine. Put the bread crumb mixture on top of the fish in the dish. Place the fish under a preheated broiler for about 8 minutes until the bread crumbs have turned a golden brown and the fish is cooked.

Sole with Tomatoes and Mushrooms

This looks very attractive with the fillets rolled up and covered with a pink sauce. For a more filling meal, lay the fish on top of baked potatoes cut in half, scooped out and re-filled with buttered mashed potato.

MAKES 4 ADULT PORTIONS

1 medium onion, peeled and chopped
2 tablespoons margarine
2 medium tomatoes, skinned, seeded and diced
3 cups mushrooms, washed and sliced

4 fillets of sole
salt and pepper
1 tablespoon tomato catsup
2 tablespoons heavy cream

Sauté the onion in the margarine until soft. Add the tomato and mushrooms and cook for 2–3 minutes. Season the fish with salt and pepper, roll up and secure with a wooden toothpick. Place the fish in a greased dish, spoon over the tomato sauce and dot with the catsup. Cook, uncovered, for 15 minutes in an oven preheated to 400°F. Remove the fish fillets, discard the toothpicks, and liquidize the sauce in a blender. Stir in the cream, then pour over the fish. Serve with mashed potatoes or rice.

Sesame Fish

This is a very quick, easy and tasty fish recipe.

MAKES 2 ADULT PORTIONS

2 fillets of flounder or sole
1 tablespoon margarine
2 teaspoons sesame seeds

2 teaspoons minced scallions
a squeeze of lemon juice

Fry the fish fillets in margarine with the sesame seeds and scallions. Cook over a low heat for 3–4 minutes, turning half-way through. Add a squeeze of lemon juice. Cut fish into small pieces.

Scrambled Fish

Vary by adding chopped tomato or grated cheese before cooking.

MAKES 1 ADULT PORTION

4 oz fillet of haddock
2 tablespoons milk
salt and pepper to taste
2 tablespoons margarine

1 egg
2 teaspoons snipped chives
2 slices wholewheat bread, toasted
and buttered

Cook the fish with half the milk, seasoning and a tiny piece of the margarine (about 4 minutes in the microwave on High or the same in a pan on top of the stove). Beat the egg, season with salt and pepper and stir in the chives. Add the flaked fish and remaining milk to the egg. Melt the remaining margarine in a saucepan, stir in the fish mixture and cook over a gentle heat for 2 or 3 minutes until it thickens, in the normal way. Serve on hot buttered toast.

Grandma's Tasty Fish Pie

This is one of my mother's recipes which is a great favorite with all the family. There is never any left the next day.

MAKES 6 ADULT PORTIONS

1 lb skinned fillets of haddock
all-purpose flour
salt and pepper
1 egg, beaten
2 slices brown bread or crisp roll,
made into bread crumbs
cooking oil
1 onion, peeled and finely chopped
1 red and 1 green bell pepper, seeded
and chopped

14 oz can tomatoes, or 2 tablespoons
tomato paste

Cheese sauce
2 tablespoons margarine
1 tablespoon all-purpose flour
1 cup milk
1¼ cups grated Cheddar cheese
⅓ cup grated Parmesan

Dip the haddock fillets into seasoned flour then into the egg and finally coat in bread crumbs. Fry in oil until golden brown on both sides. Drain off oil on paper towels, then flake the fish into small pieces and place in an ovenproof dish.

Sauté the onion in a very little oil in a frying pan for 3–4 minutes. Add the peppers and continue to cook until soft. Drain the can of tomatoes, chop the tomatoes and add to the peppers and onion. Cook for a further 3–4 minutes then season. Pour over the fish.

Make a cheese sauce with the margarine, flour and milk, stirring over a low heat until smooth and thick (see page 59). Take the saucepan off the heat and stir in just over half of the grated cheese, reserving the rest to sprinkle over the top of the fish pie.

Cover the flaked fish and tomato with the cheese sauce and top with the reserved grated Cheddar and Parmesan. Cook in an oven preheated to 350°F for 20 minutes. Brown under the broiler.

Kedgeree

I am surprised how many toddlers like the taste of smoked fish.
Both my children love smoked fish. Smoked fish is very salty,
however and can make your toddler very thirsty.

MAKES 2 ADULT PORTIONS

*8 oz smoked haddock (or canned
salmon)*
1/2 cup brown rice
2 tablespoons margarine
*1/2 small onion, peeled and finely
chopped*

1 teaspoon tomato catsup
1/2 teaspoon curry powder (optional)
1 hard-boiled egg, chopped
1 teaspoon lemon juice
1 tablespoon chopped parsley

Poach the haddock in enough water to cover for 10 minutes or until
cooked. Drain, reserving the cooking liquid. Flake the fish carefully, discarding the skin and bones. Cook the rice in the reserved
liquid, adding a little extra water if necessary (about 15 minutes).

Melt the margarine in a saucepan and fry the chopped onion until
soft but not brown. Stir in the tomato catsup and curry powder (if
used), then add all the rest of the ingredients and cook over a moder-
ate heat for about 5 minutes.

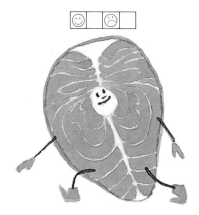

Tuna Bake with Potato Chips

MAKES 2 ADULT PORTIONS

1 tablespoon margarine
1 tablespoon all-purpose flour
1 cup milk
1 small can tuna in oil (4–6 oz),
drained and flaked

³/₄ cup button mushrooms, washed,
sliced and sautéed in a little butter
1 hard-boiled egg, chopped (optional)
pepper
1 small bag potato chips, crushed

Make a white sauce with the margarine, flour and milk (see page 59). Stir constantly, until the sauce thickens. Add the flaked tuna to this, together with the sliced mushrooms, chopped egg and a little seasoning. Add half the crushed chips and pour this mixture into a greased casserole dish. Sprinkle the remainder of the chips on top and bake in the oven preheated to 350°F for 30 minutes.

Haddock in an Orange Sauce

MAKES 2 ADULT PORTIONS

8 oz fillet of haddock, skinned
juice of 1 orange
³/₈ cup grated Cheddar cheese
2 teaspoons finely chopped parsley

1 tomato, skinned, seeded and
chopped
1 cup crushed cornflakes
¹/₂ tablespoon margarine

Put the haddock in a greased dish, cover with the orange juice, cheese, parsley, tomato and cornflakes and dot with the margarine. Cover with foil and bake at 350°F for about 20 minutes.
Flake the fish carefully, removing any bones and mash everything together with the liquid in which the fish was cooked.

Tuna Tagliatelle

This is my favorite tuna recipe.

MAKES 3 ADULT PORTIONS

1/2 onion, peeled and finely chopped
2 tablespoons margarine
15 fl oz can cream of tomato soup
1 teaspoon cornstarch
4–6 oz can tuna, drained and flaked
a pinch of mixed herbs
1 tablespoon chopped parsley
3 cups green tagliatelle
grated Parmesan cheese

Mushroom cheese sauce
1/2 onion, peeled and finely chopped
1/4 cup margarine
3/4 cup mushrooms, washed and sliced
2 tablespoons all-purpose flour
1 1/4 cups milk
1 cup grated Cheddar cheese

For the sauce, fry the onion in the margarine until transparent then add the sliced mushrooms and sauté for about 3 minutes. Add the flour and continue stirring the mixture all the time. When it is well mixed, add the milk gradually and cook, stirring, until smooth. Remove from the heat and stir in the grated cheese.

Fry the onion in the margarine until soft and stir in the tomato soup which has been thickened with the cornstarch mixed with a little cold water. Add the tuna, mixed herbs and chopped parsley.

Boil the tagliatelle in water until *al dente*, then drain. Grease a serving dish and add the tuna and tomato mixed with the noodles and then the mushroom cheese sauce. Top with grated Parmesan. Bake in an oven preheated to 350°F for 20 minutes. Brown under a hot broiler before serving.

Tuna or Salmon Gratin

If you keep a can of tuna or salmon in the larder, then it is easy to combine it with some leftover vegetables to make a tasty fish pie. The ingredients can be varied according to what you have available.

MAKES 3 ADULT PORTIONS

1½ cups button mushrooms, washed and sliced
1 tablespoon margarine
¾ cup frozen peas
4–6 oz can tuna or salmon
1 large tomato, skinned, seeded and cut into chunks
1 hard-boiled egg, chopped

Sauce
1 tablespoon margarine
1 tablespoon all-purpose flour
⅝ cup milk
¼ cup grated Cheddar cheese

Topping
2 potatoes, peeled, boiled and mashed with a little milk, margarine, salt and pepper
¼ cup grated Cheddar cheese

Fry the mushrooms in a little margarine for a couple of minutes, and cook the frozen peas until just tender. Make the sauce in the usual way, with the margarine, flour and milk, stirring over a gentle heat until it thickens (see page 59). Remove from the heat and stir in the grated cheese. Add the tuna or salmon, peas, mushrooms, tomato and chopped egg to the sauce. Pour this mixture into a greased ovenproof dish. Cover with mashed potato and top with grated cheese. Cook for 20 minutes in an oven preheated to 350°F and brown under the broiler for a couple of minutes before serving.

CHICKEN

Chicken Casserole with Tomatoes and Peppers

An easy-to-make chicken casserole which is delicious served with
rice or mashed potato.

MAKES 6 ADULT PORTIONS

*3 double chicken breasts, off the bone
and skinned
all-purpose flour
salt and pepper
cooking oil
2 onions, peeled and finely chopped
2 bell peppers (1 red, 1 green or
1 yellow), seeded and finely chopped*

*28 oz can of tomatoes
2 chicken bouillon cubes, dissolved in
³/₄ cup water
1 tablespoon each of chopped parsley
and mixed herbs
1 bay leaf
6 cups button mushrooms, carefully
washed*

Roll the chicken breasts in seasoned flour and fry them, turning
frequently, in a little oil until golden. Meanwhile fry the onion for
3–4 minutes in a little oil until soft, then add the chopped peppers and
continue to fry for another 3 minutes. Pat off any excess fat from the
cooked chicken with paper towels and drain off excess oil from the
pepper and onion.

Drain off the tomato juice and chop the tomatoes into pieces. Put
the chicken into a large casserole dish with the onion, pepper, tomato,
concentrated chicken bouillon, herbs and some seasoning. Cook in an
oven preheated to 350°F for 30 minutes. Add the button mushrooms
and continue to cook for a further 30 minutes.

Bar-B-Q Chicken

Chicken cooked in this way is slightly sweet and very succulent. It is a great favorite with my son. I use a Weber Bar-B-Q, which has a cover, thus enabling me to barbecue food all the year round, even in England.

MAKES 4–5 ADULT PORTIONS

2 lb breast of chicken, on the bone and skinned

Marinade
3 tablespoons red wine vinegar
1 tablespoon soy sauce
3/4 tablespoon Worcestershire sauce
1/2 tablespoon runny honey
black pepper

Mix all the marinade ingredients together and marinate the chicken for not less than 2 hours. Grill the chicken by whichever method you have available, basting the chicken frequently with the sauce (about 35–40 minutes). When cooked, take the chicken off the bone and cut into pieces.

Chicken Satay

These barbecued chicken skewers are fun to eat and very popular with toddlers. Help your child take the meat off the skewers, then remove the skewers – they could become dangerous in the hands of exuberant toddlers.

MAKES ABOUT 4 ADULT PORTIONS

*2 double chicken breasts, off the bone
and skinned
¹/₂ onion, peeled
¹/₂ red bell pepper, seeded
8 button mushrooms, washed*

Marinade
*¹/₄ cup light sesame oil
2 tablespoons lemon juice
1 tablespoon smooth peanut butter
3 tablespoons runny honey*

In a bowl mix together all the ingredients for the marinade. Cut the chicken, onion and pepper into chunks. Leave the chicken in the marinade for at least 2 hours. Thread the chicken, onion, pepper and mushrooms on to skewers and barbecue basting the chicken, frequently with the marinade.

☺ ☹

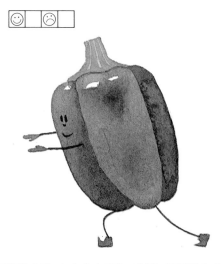

Chicken Paprika

This dish is not very spicy so don't be afraid to give it to young children. If you want to make it 'hot' for adults, substitute 1 teaspoon cayenne pepper for paprika. Serve with noodles or rice.

MAKES 4 ADULT PORTIONS

vegetable oil
2 onions, peeled and chopped
2 double breasts of chicken, on the bone and skinned
all-purpose flour
salt and pepper
1 red and 1 green bell pepper, seeded and diced

2 teaspoons paprika
2 large tomatoes, skinned, seeded and cut in small pieces
1¼ cups chicken broth (see page 62)
1 tablespoon cornstarch
¼ cup soured cream

In a heavy saucepan heat a little oil and sauté the onion until golden. Meanwhile, roll the chicken in seasoned flour then, in a separate frying pan, brown in a little oil. Drain on paper towels. Add the diced pepper, a little salt and paprika to the onion, cook for 3 minutes then add the tomatoes and the chicken broth. Cover and simmer for 5 minutes then add the chicken and cook until tender (about 20 minutes).

Remove the chicken, take it off the bone and cut the flesh into small bite-sized pieces. Mix the cornstarch with a little cold water and stir it into the sauce. Bring to a boil, stirring constantly.

Stir the soured cream into the sauce and allow it to simmer (do not let it boil) for a few minutes. Pour over the chicken.

Chicken Fillets with Mango Chutney and Apricot

This is very simple to prepare but tastes absolutely delicious. It is a great favorite with children because of the sweet and sour taste.

MAKES 2 ADULT PORTIONS

1 double chicken breast, off the bone and skinned

Sauce
1 tablespoon apricot jam
1 tablespoon mango chutney
3 tablespoons mayonnaise
1 teaspoon Worcestershire sauce
1 tablespoon lemon juice

Mix all the ingredients together for the sauce. Put the chicken into a small ovenproof dish, pour over the sauce and cover the dish with aluminum foil. Bake in an oven preheated to 350°F for 30 minutes.

☺ ☹

Stir-Fried Chicken with Vegetables and Noodles

This recipe can be made with any leftover vegetables; the choice of vegetables below can be used as a guide. As a short-cut, some supermarkets sell packets of ready prepared stir-fry vegetables. The colorful different foods are very appealing to toddlers.

MAKES 6 ADULT PORTIONS

3 single breasts of chicken, off the bone and skinned
3 tablespoons soy sauce
²/₃ cup cooked egg noodles
vegetable oil
1 small onion, peeled
2 baby leeks, trimmed
1 medium carrot, peeled

1 cup cauliflower flowerets
2 cups shredded cabbage
1¹/₂ cups bean sprouts
1¹/₂ cups oyster (or button) mushrooms, washed
1 cup snow peas, stringed
6 baby corncobs, trimmed
¹/₃ cup sesame seeds, toasted (see page 131)

Prepare the chicken in advance by cutting it into small pieces and marinating it in the soy sauce for at least 2 hours. Drain the marinade from the chicken and reserve. Cook the noodles according to the instructions on the packet then, when cooked, drain and stir in a little oil to prevent them sticking together.

Chop all the vegetables into small pieces. Put 2 tablespoons of oil in a *wok* or frying pan and, when hot, add the chopped onion and leeks. When transparent, add the chicken and cook for about 5 minutes or until the chicken is just cooked through. Add the carrot and cauliflower and cook for 2 minutes with a little of the soy sauce from the marinade. Add the rest of the vegetables and soy sauce and cook for 3–4 minutes depending on how crisp you like them. Add the noodles to the stir-fry, mix thoroughly and sprinkle with the toasted sesame seeds.

☺ ☹

Mulligatawny Chicken

This recipe has a tomato base and a mild curry flavor which children love. It has been a family favorite since I was a child and was invented by my mother. It is best served with rice and, for special occasions, you can serve *poppadums* as an accompaniment. They are available in most supermarkets.

MAKES 8 ADULT PORTIONS

1 chicken, cut into about 10 pieces, skinned
all-purpose flour
salt and pepper to taste
vegetable oil
2 medium onions, peeled and chopped
6 tablespoons tomato paste
2 tablespoons mild curry powder
2 pints chicken broth (see page 62)

1 large or 2 small apples, cored and thinly sliced
1 small carrot, peeled and thinly sliced
2 lemon slices
1/2 cup golden raisins
1 bay leaf
2 teaspoons brown sugar

Coat the chicken pieces with seasoned flour. Fry in vegetable oil until golden brown. Drain on paper towels and place in a casserole dish.

Fry the onion in a little oil until golden, then stir in the tomato paste. Add the curry powder and continue to stir for a couple of minutes over a low heat. Stir in 2 tablespoons of flour, then pour in 1½ cups of the broth, mixing well.

Add the apple, carrot, lemon slices, golden raisins, bay leaf and the rest of the broth. Season with brown sugar, salt and pepper. Pour the sauce over the chicken in the casserole, cover and cook for 1 hour in an oven preheated to 350°F. Remove the lemon slices and bay leaf; take the chicken off the bone and cut it into pieces.

Sesame Chicken Nuggets with Honey Lemon Sauce

These make great finger food. They can be served as a hot meal or they can be eaten cold on their own or cooked in the honey lemon sauce.

MAKES 8 CHICKEN NUGGETS

1 double breast of chicken, off the bone and skinned
1 egg
1 tablespoon milk
all-purpose flour
sesame seeds
1 tablespoon vegetable oil

Marinade
1 teaspoon soy sauce
¼ teaspoon salt
¼ teaspoon sugar
1 teaspoon cornstarch
1 tablespoon water

Sauce
1 tablespoon honey
2 teaspoons soy sauce
1 teaspoon freshly squeezed lemon juice

Cut each half of the chicken breast into about four pieces. Combine the ingredients for the marinade and marinate the chicken in this for at least 2 hours.

Beat the egg together with the milk and dip the chicken nuggets into the flour, then into the egg and finally coat with sesame seeds. Fry in hot oil for about 5 minutes, turning the chicken frequently, until golden brown.

Combine the ingredients for the sauce, pour this over the chicken in the frying pan and continue to cook for 2 minutes more.

Sauté of Chicken Livers with Wheatgerm

MAKES 2 ADULT PORTIONS

2 shallots, peeled and finely chopped
margarine
1/2 cup baby carrots, washed and cut
into fine strips
4 oz chicken livers

1 egg, beaten
2 tablespoons wheatgerm
1/4 cup chicken broth
(see page 62)

Fry the shallot in 2 tablespoons of margarine. After 1 minute, add the carrots and continue to fry for another minute. Dip the prepared liver into the beaten egg then coat with wheatgerm. Fry for about 3 minutes. It may be necessary to add a little more margarine to the frying pan to stop the liver from sticking. Pour over the chicken broth and simmer, covered, for a further 15 minutes or until the liver is cooked through. Chop the liver into pieces and serve with a little mashed potato.

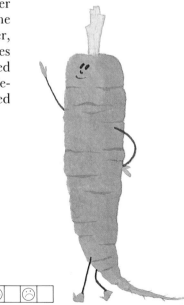

MEAT

Juicy Beefburgers

These are super moist beefburgers. Serve them with French fries
and tomato catsup for a special treat.

MAKES 8 BEEFBURGERS

1 ripe tomato, skinned and seeded
1 medium onion, peeled
1 medium potato, peeled
1 lb lean ground beef
4 tablespoons wholewheat bread
crumbs
1 tablespoon chopped parsley

1 teaspoon Vegemite dissolved in
¼ cup boiling water
black pepper
vegetable oil for frying

Topping
1 onion, peeled, finely sliced and fried
in a little oil

Grate the tomato, onion and potato in a food processor and add to
the meat. Add all the rest of the ingredients and mix well. Heat
some oil in a frying pan and shape the meat into eight patties. Fry for
about 10 minutes, browning the burgers well on each side. Serve with
the fried onion slices on top.

Cocktail Meatballs with Tomato Sauce

This is especially nice served with spaghetti and makes a great meal for the whole family. The meatballs on their own make good finger food and can be eaten either hot or cold.

MAKES 36 SMALL MEATBALLS

1 lb lean ground beef	Tomato sauce
1 onion, peeled and finely chopped	1 onion, peeled and finely chopped
1 tablespoon chopped parsley	a little margarine
1 teaspoon Vegemite mixed with a	1/2 red and green bell pepper, seeded
little boiling water	and finely chopped
1 egg, beaten	14 oz can tomatoes, drained and
salt and pepper to taste	chopped
2 thin slices white bread	2 tablespoons tomato paste
2 tablespoons milk	1 teaspoon red wine vinegar
all-purpose flour	1 tablespoon milk
1/4 cup margarine	1 tablespoon chopped basil

In a bowl, mix together the meat, chopped onion, parsley, Vegemite, beaten egg and seasoning. Trim the crust off the white bread and soak it in milk for a few minutes, then squeeze out the excess moisture. Break the bread into small pieces and add this to the ground meat. Form the mixture into small balls and roll in seasoned flour. Fry in the margarine until browned all over.

To make the tomato sauce, fry the onion in a little margarine until transparent, then add the bell pepper and fry for another 4 minutes. Add the tomatoes, tomato paste, vinegar, milk, basil and salt and pepper. Simmer for 10–15 minutes. Put the meatballs into a covered casserole dish and pour over the tomato sauce. Mix well and cook in an oven preheated to 300°F for 1 hour.

Shepherd's Pie

This is traditional British winter fare. It is very nice to make your child his very own little shepherd's pie. Let him see it, and then spoon out of the hot dish on to his plate.

MAKES 6 ADULT PORTIONS

1 onion, peeled and finely chopped
vegetable oil
1 lb lean ground beef
1/2 red and green bell pepper, seeded and finely chopped
1 tablespoon finely chopped parsley
1 cup chicken broth (see page 62)
1 teaspoon Vegemite or a bouillon cube

salt and pepper
1 1/2 cups button mushrooms, washed and sliced
a little margarine

Topping
3 cups potatoes, peeled and chopped
1 tablespoon margarine
1/4 cup milk

Fry the chopped onion in a little oil in a saucepan until golden. Meanwhile, in a frying pan, brown the ground meat. When the onions are cooked, add the chopped pepper and parsley and continue to cook for 4–5 minutes. Put meat into a food processor for 30 seconds to make it easier to chew. Add to the pan with the onion mixture and stir in the chicken broth, Vegemite and seasonings. Cook over a low heat for about 20 minutes. Meanwhile, sauté the mushrooms in a little oil and add these to the meat when it is cooked.

To make the topping, boil the potatoes in salted water for about 25 minutes. When soft, mash them together with the margarine, milk and some salt and pepper. Spread over the meat either in one large dish or individual dishes, then cook in the oven preheated to 350°F for 10 minutes. Dot the top with margarine and put under a hot broiler for about 3 minutes or until brown and crispy.

Benihana Steak

When two years old, my son loved to go to Benihana. Benihana means 'red rose' and is the name given to a chain of Japanese restaurants worldwide which specialise in *Teppan-yaki* cooking. The food is prepared in front of the customers by a Japanese chef who entertains the children.by throwing the food and his knives in the air whilst cooking! After lunch the children are entertained upstairs with a puppet show.

Needless to say this is something I am not prepared to do in my own kitchen, but I have talked to the head chef at Benihana and he has given me some easy-to-prepare Japanese recipes which are great for kids. An optional extra to these recipes is, of course, one silk kimono to be worn by Mum!

MAKES 2 ADULT PORTIONS

5 oz sirloin steak
2 tablespoons soy sauce
1/2 teaspoon sugar

2 tablespoons chopped onions
3/4 cup button mushrooms, sliced
soy or vegetable oil

Cut the steak into bite-sized cubes. Heat the soy sauce with the sugar until the sugar has dissolved. Marinate the steak in the soy sauce, sugar and chopped onion for about 30 minutes.

Drain off the soy sauce and onions and set aside. Heat the oil in a frying pan and when it is hot, fry the meat until tender. Remove the meat and fry the onion and mushrooms. Combine the steak, mushrooms and onion and serve.

Veal Stroganoff

Veal is easier than beef for your toddler to chew. This recipe is quick and easy to make and delicious. It is very nice as a family meal served with noodles and, to give it an authentic stroganoff taste, you can even add a dollop of soured cream.

MAKES 2 ADULT PORTIONS

cooking oil
1 onion, peeled and very finely chopped
1/2 red and yellow bell pepper, seeded and cut into strips
8 oz thin veal scallop, cut into strips

all-purpose flour
salt and pepper
1 1/4 cups chicken broth (see page 62)
2 cups button mushrooms, washed and sliced

Heat a little oil in a frying pan and sauté the onion for 3–4 minutes. Add the strips of bell pepper and continue to cook for 1 more minute. Roll the strips of veal in seasoned flour and cook these in the frying pan for about 3 minutes or until browned (add a little more oil if you find the veal is sticking to the pan).

Pour the chicken broth over the veal and stir in the mushrooms and some salt and pepper. Simmer, covered, for about 8 minutes.

Celery Chops

Toddlers enjoy eating chops as they can hold them in their hands.

MAKES 4 ADULT PORTIONS

4 lamb chops
vegetable oil
2 tablespoons brown sugar
1/2 teaspoon mustard powder

1 tablespoon lemon juice
a little black pepper
3 celery stalks, finely chopped
4 tablespoons tomato catsup

Sauté the chops in a little oil to brown them. In a bowl, mix together the brown sugar, mustard, lemon juice and black pepper. Brush this mixture over the chops. Sprinkle the chopped celery over the chops and pour over the tomato catsup. Bake in the oven pre-heated to 350°F for 35 minutes.

Liver and Onion

You are doing a great job if your children enjoy liver.

MAKES 1–2 ADULT PORTIONS

1/2 onion, peeled and chopped
1 tablespoon finely chopped green bell pepper
vegetable oil

2 tablespoons chopped mushrooms
1 medium tomato, skinned, seeded and chopped
4 oz calf's liver

Fry the chopped onion and pepper in a little oil until the onions are very brown. Add the chopped mushrooms and tomato and fry for another 2 minutes. Fry the liver for 1½ minutes each side. When the liver is cooked cut into small pieces and cover with the vegetables.

PASTA

Spinach Pasta Sauce

This is a delicious sauce which is good with any type of pasta.

MAKES 2 ADULT PORTIONS

*4 cups fresh, washed spinach, tough
stalks removed (or use frozen)
2 tablespoons margarine
1 tablespoon all-purpose flour*

*1 cup milk
2 tablespoons grated Parmesan cheese
a pinch of freshly grated nutmeg
salt and pepper to taste*

Cook the spinach in very little water for about 5 minutes, then drain, reserving 2 tablespoons of the cooking liquid.

Meanwhile make a white sauce with the margarine, flour and milk (see page 59). Bring to a boil, then simmer for 2–3 minutes. Add the reserved spinach liquid, together with the Parmesan and nutmeg.

Finely chop the spinach in a food processor and stir this into the sauce. Season with salt and pepper. Serve with the cooked pasta of your choice and sprinkle with a little extra Parmesan cheese.

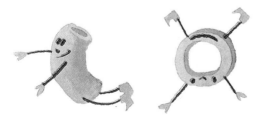

Penne with Zucchini and Cheese

Children love pasta which they can pick up with their fingers.

MAKES 4 ADULT PORTIONS

4 zucchini, sliced
5 tablespoons olive oil
2¹/₂ cups penne (tubes)

¹/₂ cup Mozzarella cheese, cubed
1 egg, beaten
¹/₄ cup grated Parmesan cheese

Fry the zucchini slices lightly in olive oil. Take care not to overcook them as they should be just tender. Cook the pasta according to instructions on the packet but make sure that it is *al dente*.

Heat a serving bowl and as soon as the pasta is cooked, drain it and pour it into the bowl. Add the cubed Mozzarella and stir well until all the cheese has melted. Add the beaten egg and zucchini, stirring quickly, then sprinkle with the Parmesan cheese. Brown under hot broiler, then serve immediately.

Macaroni Cheese with Catsup

This tasty macaroni cheese has a lovely crunchy topping.

MAKES 3 ADULT PORTIONS

2 cups macaroni
salt
1 tablespoon margarine
1 tablespoon all-purpose flour
³/₄ cup milk
¹/₄ cup grated Cheddar cheese
1 tablespoon tomato catsup

1 dessertspoon snipped chives
(optional)

Topping
2 tablespoons wholewheat bread
crumbs
¹/₄ cup grated Cheddar cheese,
a little margarine

Cook the macaroni in boiling salted water according to the instructions on the packet. Use the margarine, flour and milk to make a thick white sauce (see page 59). Remove from the heat and stir in the cheese, tomato catsup and chives, if using.

Put the macaroni into an ovenproof dish and mix with the sauce. Sprinkle over the bread crumbs and grated cheese and dot with margarine. Brown under the broiler for 2–3 minutes to make a crispy topping.

Spaghetti Primavera

Spaghetti with vegetables makes a delicious and colorful dish. Be careful not to overcook the vegetables or they will be soft and mushy.

MAKES 4 ADULT PORTIONS

2 tablespoons margarine
4 tomatoes, skinned, seeded and
chopped
1 tablespoon chopped basil
1½ cups mushrooms, washed and
sliced
¼ cup milk

1 cup each of small cauliflower and
broccoli flowerets
2 zucchini, trimmed and cut into
¼-inch slices
2 cups spaghettini or tagliolini
freshly grated Parmesan cheese

Melt the margarine in a small frying pan and fry the tomato and basil for 2 minutes. Add the mushrooms and cook for a further 3 minutes. Stir in the milk and continue to cook for 2 minutes.

Meanwhile, steam the remaining vegetables until they are just tender and cook the pasta according to the instructions on the packet.

Add the steamed vegetables to the mushrooms and tomatoes. Cook over a gentle heat for 2 minutes then add to the cooked pasta and mix well. Sprinkle with Parmesan and serve immediately.

Chicken Liver in Tomato Sauce with Pasta

This is a good recipe to encourage your child to eat liver. In fact, I have found that some young children who normally dislike liver will eat it when it is mixed up with pasta. Any pasta can be used but it is particularly appealing to young children with fusilli in three colors, which can be bought at most supermarkets.

MAKES 3 ADULT PORTIONS

½ small onion, peeled and finely chopped
vegetable oil
½ small red bell pepper, seeded and chopped
¾ cup mushrooms, washed and sliced

1 or 2 chicken livers, cleaned and sliced
2 tablespoons tomato paste
½ cup chicken broth (see page 62)
2 teaspoons chopped parsley
1½ cups pasta

Gently sauté the onion in a little oil. When it is soft and transparent, add the red pepper and mushrooms. Continue to cook for 2–3 minutes and then add the liver slices together with the tomato paste, chicken broth and chopped parsley. Cover and simmer gently for about 10 minutes or until the liver is tender. Cook the pasta according to packet instructions, drain, then pour the sauce over.

Animal Pasta Salad with Multi-Colored Vegetables

I make this recipe with multi-colored animal-shaped pasta. Toddlers love picking out all the different ingredients. It looks very attractive and colorful on a plate and can be served warm or cold. You can omit the chicken for a vegetarian dish.

MAKES 4 ADULT PORTIONS

2 cups multi-colored pasta shapes
1 single chicken breast, skinned and cut into bite-sized pieces
vegetable oil
3 baby carrots, or 1 medium carrot, cut into fine strips
1¹/₂ cups button mushrooms, washed and sliced
¹/₂ cup each of cauliflower and broccoli flowerets
3 zucchini, trimmed and sliced

¹/₂ cup chopped green beans
²/₃ cup frozen corn
¹/₂ red bell pepper, finely chopped
sugar

Dressing
2 tablespoons cider vinegar
¹/₂ teaspoon salt and a little black pepper
¹/₄ cup olive oil
2 scallions, finely sliced, or
2 tablespoons snipped chives

Cook the pasta according to the packet instructions, drain. Fry the chicken in a little oil for 2 minutes, then add the carrots and mushrooms and continue to cook for a further 5 minutes. Meanwhile steam the cauliflower, broccoli, zucchini and beans until cooked but still crisp. The cauliflower and broccoli will need a little longer than the zucchini and beans. Cook the corn and red pepper in water with a little salt and sugar for 5 minutes.

To prepare the dressing, whisk the vinegar with the salt and pepper, then whisk in the olive oil a little at a time. Add the scallions. Combine all the ingredients together and pour over the dressing.

FRUIT AND DESSERTS

Banana Split

This is simple to make and very healthy to eat. It looks attractive laid out on a plate, especially if you include some more exotic fruits like kiwi and mango.

MAKES 1 ADULT PORTION

1 banana
1 tablespoon cottage cheese

3 tablespoons of a variety of fruits,
cut into small cubes

Peel the banana and split it in half lengthwise. Lay the two halves side by side on a plate with the two ends touching one another. Spread the cottage cheese in the center of the bananas and pile the chopped fruit on top. ☺ ☹

Peach Melba Delight

A healthy alternate to this favorite ice-cream dessert.

MAKES 2 ADULT PORTIONS

⅝ cup yogurt
½ cup ricotta
1 tablespoon lemon juice
1 teaspoon superfine sugar (optional)

1 peach, skinned and cut into small
pieces
1¼ cups raspberries
1 tablespoon cornflakes, crushed

Mix the yogurt, ricotta, lemon juice and sugar. Stir in the fruit and sprinkle with crushed cornflakes.

Snow-Covered Fruit Salad

Try this combination of fruits which are all rich in Vitamin C, better than any vitamin tablets. You can make your own combination according to what is in season.

MAKES 5 ADULT PORTIONS

1 peach, skinned, pitted and cut into small pieces
1 papaya, peeled, seeded and cut into small chunks
8 strawberries, washed, hulled and cut into quarters
2 oranges, peeled, white skin removed and cut into chunks
1 tablespoon blueberries or raspberries
½ small canteloupe melon, flesh removed and cut into chunks

1 cup cherries, pitted and halved
1 small wedge of watermelon, flesh removed and cut into chunks
2 kiwi fruit, peeled and sliced juice of 1 orange

Topping
2 cups plain yogurt
2 tablespoons honey
2 tablespoons wheatgerm or muesli

Combine all the fruits together in a large bowl. Pour the orange juice over them and mix well.

Mix the yogurt with the honey and wheatgerm or muesli and pour over the fruit just before serving.

Peaches with Amaretto Biscuits

Amaretto biscuits are small round macaroons from Italy which are wrapped in pairs in tissue paper. If you cannot find them, you could substitute crushed macaroon cookies. This is very simple to make, looks very attractive and tastes delicious! (If you are making it for adults, then try substituting Amaretto liqueur for the apple juice.)

MAKES 4 ADULT PORTIONS

2 ripe peaches *³/₈ cup apple juice*
4 Amaretto biscuits *¹/₈ teaspoon almond extract*

Wash the peaches and cut them in half. Carefully remove the pits. Lay the peaches skin side down in an ovenproof dish. Place an Amaretto biscuit in the hollow of each peach. Mix together the apple juice and almond extract and pour this over the peaches. Cover the dish with aluminum foil and bake in the oven preheated to 350°F for 15–20 minutes. The peaches can be eaten hot or cold.

Apple Crumble

I like a lot of fruit in this sort of dessert so this recipe tends to have a larger proportion of fruit than topping. By using naturally sweet dessert apples instead of tart apples, you do not need to cook the apples first and you do not need to add sugar to the fruit.
As an alternate, substitute 3 cups chopped rhubarb, ⅓ cup brown sugar and the juice of a small orange for the apples and cinnamon to make rhubarb crumble. Or use the apple and blackberry mixture on page 86.

MAKES 6 ADULT PORTIONS

6 dessert apples, peeled, cored and
thinly sliced
½ teaspoon powdered cinnamon
2 tablespoons water

Crumble topping
1 cup all-purpose flour or
½ plain and ½ wholemeal
⅜ cup margarine or butter, cut into
pieces
¼ cup superfine sugar
⅔ cup rolled oats
a pinch of salt

For the crumble topping, sift the flour into a mixing bowl, add the margarine or butter pieces and cut in. Add the sugar, oats and salt and continue cutting until the mixture clings together in large crumbs.

Put the apple slices into a fairly deep round dish and add the cinnamon and water. Top with the crumble mixture and bake in the oven preheated to 350°F for 30 minutes, by which time the top of the crumble should have turned a golden brown.

Easy No-Bake Cheesecake

This is one of the most delicious cheesecakes I have tasted, and the recipe was given to me by a friend, Maureen Kerzner. It is very smooth and creamy and takes no more than 15 minutes to make. If you want to serve it to adults and impress your friends, soak the fingers in a mixture of milk and brandy instead of apple juice.

MAKES 15 ADULT PORTIONS

Base
40 Lady Fingers soaked in ¾ cup apple juice

Topping
1 packet lemon gelatin
¾ cup boiling water
1 cup evaporated milk
3 cups low-fat cream cheese
1 cup superfine sugar
1 teaspoon vanilla extract
1 cup whipping cream
powdered cinnamon

Dissolve the gelatin in the boiling water. In a large bowl, mix together the evaporated milk, cream cheese, sugar and vanilla. Stir in the cooled gelatin mixture. Beat the whipping cream until it stands up in soft peaks. Fold the cream into the gelatin mixture.

Lay half the softened fingers in the base of a 10 × 3 inch pan. Pour half the cheese mixture over the finger base, top with a layer of the remaining soaked fingers. Pour over the remaining cheese mixture and allow to set in the fridge for several hours. Dust the top with cinnamon.

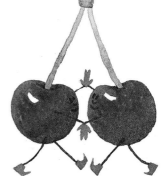

168

Cherry Pie

Make this simple delicious dessert when cherries are in season.

MAKES 6 ADULT PORTIONS

³/₄ cup all-purpose flour, sifted
¹/₄ cup superfine sugar
a pinch of salt
3 eggs

2 cups milk
3 cups cherries, pitted
2 tablespoons margarine or butter
superfine sugar for sprinkling on top

Make a well in the flour and blend in the sugar, salt and eggs. Beat in the milk gradually to a smooth batter. Spread the cherries in a greased ovenproof dish and pour over the batter. Dot margarine on top and bake at 350°F for 35–40 minutes. Sprinkle with sugar.

Grandma's Lokshen Pudding

Lokshen is vermicelli, very fine egg noodles. This easy dessert is one of my all-time favorites. For variation, add a few flaked almonds.

MAKES 8 ADULT PORTIONS

3 cups vermicelli
1 cup of golden raisins, and
1 cup of currants or raisins
1 large egg, beaten

¹/₄ cup margarine, melted
2 teaspoons brown sugar
³/₄ teaspoon cinnamon or mixed spice

Cook the vermicelli in boiling water for about 5 minutes. Mix the remaining ingredients together and then mix with the drained vermicelli. Placed in a greased shallow baking dish, dot with extra margarine and bake for 30 minutes at 300°F.

Home-made Dairy Ice Cream

Home-made ice cream is always delicious but often contains eggs, sugar and lots of heavy cream. Whipping cream has a much lower fat content than double cream or you could use full-fat plain yogurt. You may want to add a little honey or sugar to sweeten the ice cream if using all or some yogurt instead of cream. Add different flavorings or fruit purées to this basic dairy ice cream for a host of delicious yet healthy frozen desserts.

MAKES 6 ADULT PORTIONS

1 cup skim evaporated milk
2 teaspoons powdered gelatin

⁵/₈ cup whipping cream or 1 cup yogurt or ¹/₂ quantity of yogurt and ¹/₂ of cream

Chill the evaporated milk and then whisk until very thick and foamy. Dissolve the gelatin by sprinkling over 3 tablespoons of very hot water. Add the gelatin to the whisked evaporated milk, folding it in gently. Chill for 30 minutes. Whip the cream to soft peaks and fold into the whisked mixture and/or fold in the yogurt. Spoon into a freezerproof container. Freeze for 2 hours, then remove from the freezer and whisk thoroughly. Return to the freezer until firm. Soften at room temperature for 15 minutes before serving.

For variations add fruit purées or other flavors after the cream.

Peach and Redcurrant. ¹/₂ cup peach purée and 2 tablespoons of redcurrant jelly.

Pear and Ginger. ³/₄ cup pear purée and ¹/₄ teaspoon ginger.

Berry Fruit. ³/₄ cup any berry fruit purée such as strawberry, raspberry, blackberry, loganberry or a mixture. Strain before using.

Exotic Fruit. ³/₄ cup mango, papaya, litchi, pineapple, cantaloupe purée or a combination of any of these.

Halva. ³/₄ cup flaked halva.

Maple Choc Chip. 2 tablespoons maple syrup and 3 tablespoons chocolate chips.

Fruit Suckers

Suckers are always popular with children. You can buy molds with re-usable plastic sticks. Fill the molds with your chosen fruit purée or fruit juice, put the plastic sticks on top (these also serve as covers) and freeze on a level surface in the freezer. Dip the mold into warm water when you want to get a sucker out. Or use plastic or paper cups, cover with foil, pierce with a wooden stick and let it almost touch the bottom of the cup.

You can make your own fruit purées from fresh fruits in season or you can use natural fruit juices as the basis of your suckers. Sweeten to taste with sugar or honey and stir plain yogurt into fresh fruit purée for a frozen yogurt sucker. These pure ingredients are much better for your child than commercial suckers many of which are full of additives, colorings and sugar.

My son Nicholas, when two years old, had fairly sophisticated taste and developed a penchant for passion-fruit suckers (as did his father, who goes straight for the freezer after supper!). Try also blackcurrant juice, pineapple juice, and sparkling apple juice. Two-tone suckers are fun. Half-fill the molds with purée of one color, freeze then pour over a purée of a contrasting color.

Fruit Salad Suckers

MAKES 6 SUCKERS

1 apple, peeled and cored
1 pear, peeled and cored
1 orange, peeled and segmented

1 small banana
½ cup freshly squeezed orange juice

Combine in a blender or processor and blend until smooth. Pour into molds and freeze.

BAKING FOR TODDLERS

Thumbprint Jelly Cookies

So called because you stick your thumb in the middle of the dough to make a hollow for the jelly. The deeper you stick your thumb the more jelly you get. Use your child's favorite jelly or make different flavor jelly cookies.

MAKES 25 SMALL COOKIES

1/2 cup butter
1/4 cup superfine sugar
1 egg yolk
1/2 teaspoon almond extract

1 1/2 cups all-purpose flour
pinch of salt
strawberry jelly or a selection of different jellies

Beat the butter with the sugar, then blend in the egg yolk and almond extract. Gradually add the flour and salt and mix to a dough. Take walnut-sized pieces of dough, flatten slightly and press your thumb in the center to leave an indentation. Place on a cookie sheet lined with non-stick baking paper. Fill the indentations with half a teaspoon of jelly and bake in an oven preheated to 350°F for 10 minutes.

☺ ☹

Tea-Time Apple Treat

This is a lovely moist cake with lots of apple slices on top. Cut this cake into squares and watch them vanish at your child's party.

MAKES 12 SQUARES

⅓ cup packed brown sugar
1⅓ cups all-purpose flour
1 teaspoon baking powder
a pinch of salt
1 egg
¼ cup vegetable oil
½ cup apple purée (see page 24)
¼ cup apple or vanilla yogurt
½ teaspoon vanilla extract

Topping
3 dessert apples peeled, cored and finely sliced
1 teaspoon powdered cinnamon

Glaze
4 tablespoons apricot preserve
1 tablespoon water
1 tablespoon lemon juice

Mix all the dry ingredients together in a bowl. Beat the egg with the oil, apple purée, yogurt and vanilla. Add the apple purée mixture to the dry ingredients and stir until blended.

Pour the batter into a greased shallow rectangular cake pan, 10 x 6 inches and arrange the apple slices in lines over it. Sprinkle the cinnamon over the apples and bake in an oven preheated to 350°F for 35 minutes.

For the apricot glaze, put the ingredients in a small pan and cook over a low heat for 1 minute. Strain and brush the glaze over the apple slices.

Candy Cup Cakes

These little cakes can be frozen, best done before they are frosted. They are ideal for a birthday celebration, but you might find the children are more interested in picking off the candies than they are in eating the cakes!

MAKES 24 CAKES

1/2 cup sweet butter
5/8 cup sugar
2 eggs
1/2 teaspoon vanilla extract
2 cups cake flour
2 teaspoons baking powder
1/4 teaspoon salt
5 tablespoons milk
1 cup raisins (optional)
1 packet candy-coated chocolate beans

Chocolate frosting
1 square chocolate
2 tablespoons sweet butter
1 cup powdered sugar, sifted
1 teaspoon milk
Cream cheese frosting
1/4 cup sweet butter
2 cups powdered sugar
1 teaspoon vanilla extract
1/2 cup cream cheese

Cream butter and sugar together until light and fluffy, then beat in the eggs one at a time. Add the vanilla. Sift the dry ingredients together and add to the mixture, a little at a time, alternating with the milk. If you are using raisins, add them to the batter. Half fill little paper cups set into cup-cake pans and bake in an oven preheated to 400°F for 15 minutes.

I like to make two different colored frostings, so I use chocolate and then a pale cream cheese frosting. If you prefer, make a simple glaze frosting with powdered sugar and water or juice, divide into two before you add the coloring, and then use different colors for each half.

For the chocolate frosting, melt the chocolate in a double boiler. Beat the butter with a fork until soft, then stir in the sugar a little at a time, adding a little milk to make the frosting thinner. Stir in the melted chocolate, mix thoroughly and spread the frosting over some of the cakes. (If too thick to spread, add a little more milk.) Put a few candy-coated chocolate beans on top of the frosting for decoration.

For the cream cheese frosting, beat the butter, sugar and vanilla until crumbly. Stir in the cream cheese. Do not over beat or it will become watery. Spread over the cakes and decorate with candy-coated chocolate beans.

Bran Muffins with Apples and Raisins

These are absolutely delicious and very healthy too; they never last long in our house!

MAKES ABOUT 15 MUFFINS

¹/₂ cup vegetable oil
2 tablespoons honey
2 tablespoons maple syrup
³/₄ cup milk
³/₄ cup apple juice
2 eggs, beaten

2 cups self-rising flour
1 cup bran
2 tablespoons baking powder
¹/₂ teaspoon salt
2 apples, peeled and grated
1¹/₂ cups raisins

Mix together the oil, honey and maple syrup. Add the milk, apple juice and beaten eggs. In another bowl mix the flour, bran, baking powder and salt together. Combine the liquid ingredients with the dry ingredients then fold in the grated apple and raisins. Spoon the batter into muffin cups and bake in the oven preheated to 350°F for 30 minutes.

Yogurt Processor Cake

This cake has a lovely flavor and a very moist texture. It takes no more than 5 minutes to prepare. If you wish, you can make it in two round cake pans instead of one, and sandwich them together with the cream cheese frosting from page 174.

MAKES 8 ADULT PORTIONS

scant $^3/_4$ cup sugar
1 cup vegetable oil
1 cup plain set yogurt
2 eggs

$2^1/_4$ cups cake flour
3 teaspoons baking powder
2 teaspoons vanilla extract
powdered sugar

Grease a 10-inch round tube pan. In a blender or food processor, mix the sugar with the oil, then add the yogurt and mix. Blend with the eggs, flour, baking powder and vanilla. Pour into the prepared pan and bake at 325–350°F for 55 minutes. Sprinkle the top with sugar when cold.

☺	☹	

White Chocolate Button Cookies

These are so easy to make and are really delicious. Baked for only 12 minutes, they should be quite soft when they are taken out of the oven so that when they cool down they are lovely and moist.

MAKES 20 COOKIES

$^1/_2$ cup sweet butter or margarine at room temperature
$^1/_2$ cup superfine sugar
$^1/_2$ cup lightly packed brown sugar
1 egg
1 teaspoon vanilla extract

$1^1/_2$ cups all-purpose flour
$^1/_2$ teaspoon baking powder
$^1/_4$ teaspoon salt
1 cup white chocolate buttons
$^1/_2$ cup pecans or walnuts, chopped (optional)

Beat the butter together with the sugars. With a fork, beat the egg together with the vanilla and add this to the butter mixture.

In a bowl, mix together the flour, baking powder and salt. Add this to the butter and egg mixture and blend well.

Break the chocolate buttons into smaller pieces with a rolling pin or in a food processor, and stir these together with the nuts (if used) into the batter.

Put the batter into the fridge for about 40 minutes to harden. Line several cookie sheets with non-stick baking paper and roll the batter into walnut-sized balls. Put these on to the sheets, spaced well apart, and bake in an oven preheated to 375°F for 12 minutes. Take carefully off the baking paper and let them cool.

Chewy Muesli Squares

Give these to your child as a healthy treat.

MAKES 20 SMALL SQUARES

¹/₂ cup margarine or butter
1 tablespoon honey
1 tablespoon malt extract
¹/₂ teaspoon vanilla extract
¹/₂ teaspoon bicarbonate of soda
¹/₃ cup unsweetened muesli

¹/₃ cup oats
²/₃ cup dried shredded coconut
¹/₄ cup sesame seeds
¹/₃ cup golden raisins
1 tablespoon demerara sugar

Melt the margarine together with the honey and malt extract in a saucepan, then add the vanilla and bicarbonate of soda. Mix all the remaining ingredients in a bowl, pour in the melted mixture, and stir well.

Put the mixture into a 7-inch square baking pan, and bake in the oven preheated to 350°F for 30 minutes.

Funny Shape Cookies

Cookie cutters come in all sorts of weird and wonderful shapes. I use a gingerbread cutter and animal cutouts and my son can't wait to get his hands on the cookies. I get a running commentary as to which piece of the anatomy he has just eaten!

MAKES 15–20 COOKIES
DEPENDING ON SIZE OF CUTTERS

1/2 cup wholewheat flour
1 cup all-purpose flour
1/2 cup semolina
1/4 teaspoon each ground ginger,
cinnamon, salt

3/8 cup margarine or butter
1 medium ripe banana
1 1/2 tablespoons maple sirup
cream cheese for spreading
a few raisins

Put the flours, semolina, ginger, cinnamon and salt into a mixing bowl and cut in the margarine. Mash the banana well with the maple sirup and stir into the mixture to make a smooth pliable dough.

Roll out on a lightly floured surface and cut into shapes with cookie cutters. Bake on lightly greased cookie sheets in an oven preheated to 400°F for 20 minutes until golden and firm. Cool on a wire rack.

If you wish, spread the cooled cookies with cream cheese, marking with a fork to represent the various animal's fur. Use pieces of raisin for eyes and noses. ☺ ☹

Cheese Pretzels

These are delicious and great fun to make. Your children will enjoy helping you twist the pretzels into different shapes. You can even make letters of the alphabet and spell your child's name!

MAKES 20–30 PRETZELS

3 teaspoons dried yeast
1¹/₄ cups warm water
4 cups all-purpose flour

1¹/₂ cups grated Cheddar cheese
1 egg, beaten
sesame seeds

Dissolve the yeast in the warm water. Stir in the flour and grated cheese. Knead the dough with your hands on a floured board. Break off small pieces of dough and roll into long strands of about 12 inches in length and twist into shapes. Put the pretzels on a baking sheet lined with non-stick baking paper, brush with beaten egg and sprinkle with sesame seeds. Bake for 20 minutes in the oven preheated to 475°F.

HEALTHY SNACKS

Fruit Snacks

Wash fruit well. Peel, core, seed or pit and trim as needed.

Bananas, whole or cut into pieces

Chunks of peeled and cored apples

Chunks of pear

Orange, mandarin or clementine segments with as much of the white skin removed as possible (make sure there are no seeds)

Kiwi fruit, peeled and sliced

Strawberries, hulled and halved

Seedless grapes, skinned for babies under one year

Melon, peeled and cut into bite-sized pieces

Peaches, skinned and sliced

Mango, peeled and sliced

Papaya, peeled, seeds removed and cut in thick slices

Raspberries, washed carefully

Litchis, peeled and pitted (toddlers can easily choke on litchi pits)

Pineapple, peeled and cut into chunks

Dried fruit (apricots, prunes, raisins etc). If too tough soak in boiling water

Chocolate-Dipped Fruit

A very appealing way of giving fruit to children is to melt some dark chocolate in a double boiler, dip the tip of the fruit piece into the chocolate and pierce the fruit with a toothpick. Stick the toothpicks with the fruit into an orange and put this into the fridge to allow the chocolate to harden. Strawberries, pineapple chunks and orange or tangerine segments are especially nice. Remember to remove the toothpicks before giving the fruit to your child.

Whole bananas can be coated in chocolate. Place on waxed paper and freeze or chill until the chocolate has set.

If you are worried about your child having too much chocolate, use carob as a substitute.

Vegetable Snacks

As with fruit, wash, peel, trim, and seed as appropriate.

Toddlers love to dip raw vegetables into a sauce and a nicely arranged selection of crudités is great for a toddler who is teething. Try some of the simple but delicious dip recipes that follow. Think also about things like *hummous* – made from garbanzo beans and sesame paste. This can be bought in most supermarkets. Or curd cheese mixed with a little tomato paste makes a nice creamy dip.

Carrots and cabbage, grated or chopped, mixed with a little mayonnaise and raisins, makes a simple and nutritious snack piled on to lettuce leaves.

Cheese Snacks

Cheese makes an ideal snack for toddlers. Try using a cookie cutter to make animal shapes from slices of cheese. Edam, Monterey Jack and Swiss are particular favorites with most children. Individual cheeses like the small round Babybel and the wrapped triangles of cheese are ideal as well.

Cottage cheese is also popular, plain or simply mixed with something like chopped pineapple. You could also make a scoopful of cheese into a ball, accompany it with a scoopful of grated apple mixed with raisins, and surround it with a selection of mixed fruit chopped very small. This makes a nutritious, non-fattening snack which children love.

Cottage Cheese Dip

MAKES 4 ADULT PORTIONS

½ cup cottage cheese
2 tablespoons cream cheese
Worcestershire sauce to taste

2 teaspoons chopped scallions or chives
salt and pepper to taste

Mix all the ingredients together. Serve with a selection of vegetables cut into sticks or strips of pitta bread to dip in.

Green Goddess Dip

MAKES 10 ADULT PORTIONS

1 avocado
¹/₄ cucumber, diced
6 cherry tomatoes, or 2 small
tomatoes, chopped very small
¹/₂ small red bell pepper, seeded and
diced (optional)

¹/₄ small onion, peeled and finely
chopped
2 tablespoons plain yogurt
a squeeze of lemon juice
salt and pepper to taste

Cut the avocado in half, pit, and scoop the flesh out of the skin. Mash it together with the rest of the ingredients.

Rice Crispie Cheese Balls

Your toddler will enjoy helping to shape the dough into balls.

MAKES 12 BALLS

³/₄ cup flour
¹/₄ cup margarine
¹/₂ teaspoon mustard powder
¹/₄ cup grated Cheddar cheese

¹/₂ cup grated Parmesan cheese
1¹/₂ cups Rice Crispies
1 egg, beaten
¹/₃ cup sesame seeds

Cream together the flour, margarine, mustard and cheeses. Add the rice crispies and shape the dough with your hands into small balls. Dip the balls into beaten egg, roll in sesame seeds and bake for 20 minutes in an oven preheated to 350°F.

Home-Made Fast-Food Pizza

A delicious, easy-to-make pizza, a supper time treat. The Bel Paese
cheese gives it a wonderful flavor but you can substitute
Mozzarella.

MAKES 2 ADULT PORTIONS

1 scallion, finely sliced
2 tomatoes, skinned, seeded and
chopped
4 button mushrooms, washed and
sliced

margarine
2 teaspoons tomato paste
2 teaspoons chopped basil
¼ French stick
¼ cup Bel Paese cheese, sliced

Sauté the scallion, tomatoes and mushrooms in a little margarine
for 2–3 minutes then stir in the tomato paste and basil.

Cut the bread in half and spread a little margarine on both halves.
Spread the tomato mixture over the bread and put the cheese slices on
top. Cook under a hot broiler for 3–4 minutes until golden and
bubbling.

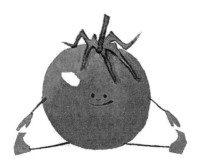

Stuffed Eggs

Cut hard-boiled eggs in half lengthwise and cut a thin sliver off the base of each half so that they stand firm. Fill with finely mashed yolks, mixed with a very small quantity of one of the following.

chopped cucumber, lettuce, tomato, and mayonnaise

OR

cottage cheese and chives

OR

poached salmon and mayonnaise

finely chopped chicken and tomato catsup

OR

canned salmon or tuna, mayonnaise and chopped scallion

Top Hat Egg

This is a great snack to give children for a special supper.

MAKES 1 ADULT PORTION

1 thick slice of bread
a little butter or margarine
1 egg

1 slice of tomato
1/4 cup grated Cheddar cheese

With a small glass or egg cup, press out a small round from the center of the bread. Fry the holed slice of bread in some butter for a few seconds on each side, then break the egg carefully into the hole in the bread. When the egg is almost cooked, place the slice of tomato on top and turn the bread back over carefully. Fry the tomato for a few seconds at the same time as the cut-out round of bread. Put the slice of bread under a hot broiler with the circle of bread on top of the tomato, and sprinkle with cheese. Broil until golden brown.

Savory French Toast

This makes excellent finger food and can be served with boiled or scrambled egg to make a complete meal.

MAKES 1 ADULT PORTION

1 slice of wholewheat bread
¹/₂ teaspoon Vegemite

1 egg
a little butter or margarine

Thinly spread the Vegemite on both sides of the bread. Beat the egg and pour it on to a flat plate. Soak the bread in the egg. Meanwhile melt a little butter in a frying pan, then fry the bread until golden on both sides. Cut the bread into fingers, removing the crusts if your child prefers.

Sandwiches

Sandwiches can come in all shapes and sizes. Try making animal-shaped sandwiches using a cookie cutter. Pinwheel sandwiches are very appealing too (see page 186). Toasted sandwiches are a meal in themselves and it is well worth investing in a toasted sandwich maker which seals the bread.

Try using lots of different breads: small round pitta bread, slit and stuffed with salad; raisin bread; open sandwiches on bridge rolls; bagels (excellent for a toddler to chew on when he is teething); French bread; pumpernickel bread (which is black); or even a sandwich where one side is white and one side is brown.

Presentation is very important. A child is more likely to eat something that looks appealing. Sprinkle the sandwiches with shredded lettuce or decorate with thinly serrated vegetables or make your sandwiches into little trains or boats. It doesn't take long and it's fun to do. I think you will find that a lot of toddlers will reach out for your sandwiches.

On the following pages are some suggestions for sandwich fillings. Your toddler will soon let you know his preferences!

Pinwheel Sandwiches

Ideally the bread for pinwheel sandwiches should be very thin. You can either thinly slice the bread yourself, or you can flatten slices with a rolling pin. If you don't flatten the bread first, it will not be pliable enough to roll without breaking. Cut off all the crusts, and spread the bread evenly with softened butter or margarine and the desired filling (which should be fairly smooth and creamy). Roll up slices with the filling on the inside and cut into slices to make little pinwheels.

You can even make a variegated pinwheel sandwich by rolling one brown and one white slice of bread (which have both been spread with different but complementary fillings) together.

Peanut butter and raspberry jelly
Peanut butter and mashed banana
Peanut butter and apple purée
Peanut butter, grated apple and toasted sesame seeds (or chopped raisins)
Cream cheese, Vegemite and shredded lettuce

Cream or curd cheese, toasted sesame seeds and grated cucumber

Cream cheese and crushed pineapple (or fruit purée)

Cream cheese and cucumber

Cream cheese and crushed cornflakes

Cream cheese in raisin bread with strawberry jelly

Cream cheese in a bagel with slices of smoked salmon

Cream cheese with chopped dried apricots

Cream cheese and redcurrant jelly

Cottage cheese with avocado and lemon juice

Cheese and chutney

Grated cheese with grated apple and pear

Plain ricotta and raisins

Chopped hard-boiled egg, watercress and mayonnaise

Egg mayonnaise with a little curry powder

Chopped hard-boiled eggs with mashed sardines

Tuna mayonnaise and cucumber

A small can of tuna or salmon with 3 tablespoons tomato catsup

Tuna or salmon salad

Canned salmon, chopped egg and mayonnaise

Chopped chicken, mayonnaise and yogurt with a little curry powder and raisins

Chicken or turkey with chutney

Grilled chicken liver, mashed with fried onions and hard-boiled egg

Chocolate spread and banana

Open Toasted Sandwiches

Toast the bread first, then spread with the topping and put under a hot grill until cooked.

Cheese and tomato

Grated cheese and apples with a few raisins

Canned sardines in tomato sauce

Chicken in béchamel sauce

TODDLER MEAL PLANNER

	Breakfast	Lunch	Early Supper	Dinner
Day 1	Fruity Swiss Muesli Yohurt Fruit	Juicy Beefburgers and vegetables Apple Crumble and custard sauce or ice cream	Animal Pasta Salad with Multi-Colored Vegetables Home-Made Ice Cream or frozen yogurt	Miniature sandwiches Yogurt Fruit
Day 2	Cheese on toast Fruit Compote	Grandma's Tasty Fish Pie Fruit	Top-Hat Egg Fruit	Chicken and Apple Balls and vegetables Snow-Covered Fruit Salad
Day 3	French Toast Apple Purée Ricotta	Veal Stroganoff and rice Baked Bananas	Gefilte Fish Balls with salad or raw vegetables in dip Fruit	Toasted sandwich Peach Melba Delight
Day 4	Mixed Cereal Muesli Scrambled egg	Tasty Peanut Rissoles Animal Gelatin and Home-Made Ice Cream	Chicken and Apple Balls Snow-Covered Fruit Salad	Spaghetti Primavera Ricotta and Fruit
Day 5	Raisin Bran Muffin Banana Split	Shepherd's Pie and vegetables Grandma's Lokshen Pudding	Fish in Creamy Mushroom Sauce Fruit Gelatin Fruit	Tasty Peanut Rissoles Fruit Yogurt
Day 6	Cornflakes with Apple Yogurt Fruit	Tuna Tagliatelle Fruit	Liver Casserole and vegetables Tea-Time Apple Treat	Miniature sandwiches Ricotta and Fruit
Day 7	Cheese Scramble and toast Fruit	Bar-B-Q Chicken or Stir-Fried Chicken Apple Crumble and Home-Made Ice Cream	Stuffed Potato Fruit Gelatin Fruit	Gratin of Sole Ratatouille Yogurt

These meal charts show you how to plan ahead and cook for the whole family together.

FAMILY MEAL PLANNER

	Breakfast	*Lunch*	*Dinner*
Day 1	Fruity Swiss Muesli Yogurt	Animal Pasta Salad with Multi-Colored Vegetables	Juicy Beefburgers, vegetables and potato Apple Crumble and custard sauce or ice cream
Day 2	Cheese on toast Fruit Compote	Chicken and Apple Balls and vegetables	Grandma's Tasty Fish Pie and vegetables Snow-Covered Fruit Salad
Day 3	French toast	Tasty Fish Pie or Gefilte Fish Balls with salad Fruit	Veal Stroganoff with rice and salad Home-Made Ice Cream or yogurt and fruit
Day 4	Scrambled egg	Tasty Peanut Rissoles or Gefilte Fish Balls or Chicken and Apple Balls Fruit salad	Spaghetti Primavera Tasty Peanut Rissoles Fruit Gelatin and Home-Made Ice Cream
Day 5	Raisin Bran Muffins	Fish in Creamy Mushroom Sauce and vegetables	Shepherd's Pie and vegetables or salad Grandma's Lokshen Pudding
Day 6	Cornflakes and Yogurt	Tuna Tagliatelle Fresh fruit	Liver Casserole and potato Tea-Time Apple Treat and Home-Made Ice Cream
Day 7	Cheese Scramble Toast and Fruit	Bar-B-Q Chicken or Stir-Fried Chicken and Vegetables Apple Crumble and Home-Made Ice Cream	Gratin of Sole Ratatouille

INDEX

Page numbers in light type denote additional recipes containing the given ingredient

ACKNOWLEDGMENTS

I am indebted to the following people for their help and advice during the writing of this book.

Dr Stephen Herman FRCP, Consultant Pediatrician, Central Middlesex Hospital, London, England.
Margaret Lawson, Senior Lecturer in Pediatric Nutrition, Institute of Child Health, University of London, England.
Professor Charles Brook, Consultant Pediatric Endocrinologist, Middlesex Hospital, London, England.
Dr Sam Tucker FRCP, Consultant Pediatrician, Hillingdon Hospital, London, England.
Jacky Bernett, Community Dietician.
Dr Tim Lobstein, specialist in children's food and nutrition at The London Food Commission.
Carol Nock SRN FCN, Midwife.

Kathy Morgan, State Registered Health Visitor.
My mother, Evelyn Etkind, for all her encouragement in writing this book.
David Karmel, for his patience in teaching me how to use a computer.
Beryl Lewsey for her enthusiasm and hard work.
Ros Edwards, Ian Jackson, Susan Fleming, Fiona Eves and Elaine Partington of Eddison Sadd.
Dr Irving Etkind, for his help in research.
Jane Hamilton, my nanny, for restraining my children from wiping out my manuscript on the computer!
And, most important of all, my husband Simon, my chief guinea pig, for all his support.

The Author

Annabel Karmel is a busy working mother with two small children, Nicholas and Lara. Her fascination for food was stimulated by studying at the Cordon Bleu School of Cookery and, since the birth of her children, she has thoroughly researched all aspects of feeding babies and children, to cut through the often confusing and conflicting advice given to mothers on the subject. A classically trained harpist, Annabel has had a glittering musical career. At the age of sixteen, she won a scholarship to the Royal Conservatoire of Music in the Hague and subsequently studied at the Royal College of Music in London, but it was through light, popular music recitals that Annabel really made her mark. She is also a singer and an actress and has made numerous television appearances. Annabel lives in London with her husband, Simon, and family.